Praise for
How to Cope with Stress after Trauma

"I started reading the manuscript for this book because Anna Goodwin asked me to see how she was utilizing my poem "The Healing Wall" throughout the book. She also asked me to share my honest response as a veteran to what she was saying. It took less than three pages for me to realize I wasn't reading a book about someone else with PTS, I was reading about me! That realization caught me off guard. And in so many unexpected ways, this book has changed my life. I know it will do the same for you. Every veteran (and your family members), regardless of the war in which you served and regardless of the experience you had in that war, needs to read this book. I know you and those who love you will be as grateful as I am that you did."

—Patrick Overton, Ph.D. in communications, and Vietnam veteran
Author of *Rebuilding the Front Porch of America: Essays on the Art of Community Making*

"This book offers our veterans and their loved ones a path towards resilience and healing. It is a strong reminder that we cannot always choose what happens to us but we can practice choosing how we respond, and how we respond to the challenges after trauma can make all the difference. The author's perspective and approach are well informed and reveal the depth of her experience."

—Dante Rumore, MSW, post-war readjustment therapist and Marine Corps veteran

"My experience with Post Traumatic Stress is different from most others. Although I am a retired U.S. Marine, I never saw combat. My trauma came in Los Angeles during Operation Desert Storm, when I had the heart-wrenching duty of informing a young wife that her Marine had been killed in the war. My response, like so many others, was to bury my emotions. *Deep!* How dare I consider my own feelings when a brother Marine had made the ultimate sacrifice and left a shattered family behind and I was alive!? Years later my emotions erupted to the surface and sent me on a years-long journey of ups and downs that continues yet today. It was only in recent months, through the interaction with the author, that I discovered that I have been dealing with Post Trauma Stress for over 23 years. I tell my story to show that PTS appears in countless forms and is all too often cloaked in shadows of misunderstanding and denial. This book is a beautiful weave of human stories, scientific research, and insightful, practical guidance to bring trauma out of the shadows and to help veterans and those who care about them to begin the healing process."

—Dr. Mark William Cochran, holistic health practitioner and speaker
Author of *Oby's Wisdom: A Caveman's Simple Guide to Holistic Health and Well-being*

"Anna Goodwin has written an extremely important book for friends and families, and most of all for veterans and anyone who has been affected by a crisis or trauma. She artfully describes the challenge of responding to trauma in the most effective and accessible way to achieve health and wholeness. I am excited to use Anna's book in my psychotherapy practice working with healing emotional wounds."
—Neil Bricco, M.S., LCPC, psychotherapist
Author of *Wisdom of the Wound: Discovering a Path to Wholeness*

"I have found in my personal and professional experience, many people have PTS and PTSD symptoms. These symptoms are often misunderstood or undetected and often go untreated for lack of understanding on the part of family, friends as well as denial on the part of the individual. PTSD symptoms impact a person's behavior and interaction with others, as well as their ability to function on a daily basis. Anna has written an excellent book that is very helpful for individuals suffering from stress after a trauma as well as families, friends, and professionals to assist in understanding and treating PTSD."
—Kathy Crawford, LCSW, psychotherapist in private practice

"Anna Goodwin has written an easily read, helpful and thoroughly authoritative guide. It should be read by all those who've experienced battle or other trauma and by all who come in contact with them."
—Jim Minard, Sleep Researcher

Hi Jim,
Thanks so much for reading the manuscript & the Testimonial.
all the very best,

Non-Fiction Books

Also by E. Anna Goodwin

Sandplay Therapy: A Step-by-Step Manual
for Psychotherapists of Diverse Orientations
Barbara L. Boik and E. Anna Goodwin
published by W.W. Norton (2000)

E Anna Goodwin

HOW TO COPE WITH STRESS AFTER TRAUMA:

ESPECIALLY FOR VETERANS, THEIR FAMILIES, AND FRIENDS

What you need to know to help yourself
or someone you love

E. ANNA GOODWIN, M.S., NCC

Bitterroot Mountain Publishing

Hayden, Idaho

How to Cope with Stress After Trauma:
Especially for Veterans, Their Families, and Friends

© 2014 by E. Anna Goodwin

All names and identifying characteristics of clients described in this book have been changed.

Published by Bitterroot Mountain Publishing LLC
9030 N. Hess Ave., Suite 331 Hayden, Idaho 83835

Interior design by Jera Publishing

Cover design by Jason Orr

Authors website: www.anaparkergoodwin.com

All rights reserved. This book or parts thereof, may not be reproduced in any form without permission, except by a reviewer who may quote brief passages in a review to be printed in magazines, newspapers, or on the web.

The ideas, procedures, and suggestions in this book are intended to supplement, not replace, the medical and psychological advice of trained professionals. The author and publisher disclaim any liability arising directly or indirectly from the use of this book.

For permission to reproduce excerpts of this publication please contact: Bitterroot Mountain Publishing at http://bitterrootmountainpublishing.com

For information about special discounts for bulk purchases, please contact: Bitterroot Mountain Publishing at http://bitterrootmountainpublishing.com

Library of Congress Control Number: 2013922157
ISBN: 978-1-940025-10-0

Printed in the United States of America

10 9 8 7 6 5 4 3 2 1

1. Post Trauma Stress—Recovery 2. Cope with stress—After trauma 3. Anxiety and depression—After stress 4. Veterans and Families—PTS Recovery I. Title.

This book is dedicated in loving memory to my husband Ronald H. Goodwin, a former military officer, who passed away in August 2014. He helped me with the research and editing of the book. But most of all his passion to help the veterans he cared about so much, continuously encouraged me to write this book and make sure it was published. Thank you dearest Ron.

Contents

Introduction 1
Whom is this book for? 4
How to use this book 8
Post Traumatic Stress Test 13
Where To Get Help 17

PART ONE: Information about Stress after a Trauma 19

What Are Post Traumatic Stress (PTS)
    and Post Traumatic Stress Disorder (PTSD)? 20

A definition of PTS and PTSD 26

Where does the diagnosis of PTSD originate? ... 30

What types of trauma can cause severe stress? ... 31

What qualifies as an unusual and/or severe trauma? ... 34

Are some people more vulnerable to stress
    after a trauma than others? 37

How prevalent are PTS and PTSD? 42

What are the symptoms of PTS and PTSD? 49

What happens in the brain and body during
    and after a severe trauma? 59

Which military personnel are most affected
    by PTS or PTSD in War? 66

PART TWO: Twenty Steps to Help You Heal 71

It's time to deal with your trauma 73

Profile of a Resilient Person 74
Step One: Become stable. 77
Step Two: Remain connected to others. 89
Step Three: Empower yourself. 99
Step Four: Learn to relax. III
Step Five: Become aware of yourself. 116
Step Six: Check with a doctor to see
   whether medications can help. 124
Step Seven: Change your thinking. 129
Step Eight: Change unwanted behaviors 145
Step Nine: Work with your emotions
   ("energy in motion"). 151
Step Ten: Reconnect spiritually. 170
Step Eleven: Deal with memories. 181
Step Twelve: Take responsibility for yourself. 198
Step Thirteen: Deal with alcohol and drug addictions. 204
Step Fourteen: Use your creativity. 209
Step Fifteen: Have fun. Laugh. Learn to play again. 215
Step Sixteen: Spend time in nature. 217
Step Seventeen: Work with your physical body. 220
Step Eighteen: Rebuild your purpose in life. 233
Step Nineteen: Explore new technologies 238
Step Twenty: Try some special techniques. 241
Conclusion 247

PART THREE: For Families and Friends 249
Introduction to Families and Friends 251
What you can do to help the veteran you love. 254

What you need to do to take care of yourself............270
What your children need............................278

The Healing Wall (Complete Poem)....................283
Suggested Readings..................................290
Acknowledgements....................................293
About the author....................................295

Introduction

If you are a veteran—or a veteran's friend or family member—this book is for you.

Why did I write a book to help veterans and their families deal with the trauma faced in war? As a former psychotherapist, an important part of my work has been building an understanding of the unique issues veterans face. But on a more personal level, I knew a man who was severely traumatized by war. I'd like to tell you about his experiences, but I can't. Why? Because he never spoke of them. He never admitted, maybe not even to himself, that something had happened that changed him forever. He did his best to hide his emotions, but regardless of how hard he tried to repress his war experiences, his wife and two children could tell when the memories flashed. Sometimes he screamed out in the night and walked the floor. After those nights he became withdrawn, anxious, and depressed. He wouldn't speak to anyone for days. Then he would burst into uncontrollable rages for what seemed no reason. There were times his family worried he would hurt someone or himself.

This man lived with the trauma of war most of his life. How do I know that the story is true? He was my father, and I was his youngest daughter. Often I felt torn inside, wondering if I was somehow to blame for his struggles. I wished

I could help, but I did not know what to do. As my father suffered day after day, so did my mother, my sister, and I.

Eventually my father did receive some help, albeit inadvertently. Because he had lost much of his hearing in one ear, he sought out a well respected surgeon who replaced his eardrum. During my father's appointments, the doctor noticed his shaking hands and agitated manner and asked him what was going on. My father said, "Nothing," as do so many people who carry the stress from a severe trauma. But the surgeon understood. He gave my father a prescription for Valium. That little white pill felt like a miracle, both to him and to our family. Fortunately he never abused the drug.

My father passed away several years ago, still not able to admit that his problems stemmed from the war. Did it matter that he could never accept what had happened to him? I don't know. He was an ardent rancher who loved the earth and spent most of his time working alone on acres and acres of land. I knew him as a somber man who rarely mingled in large groups. But according to his sisters, before the war he had been a talkative, outgoing youth who loved to laugh and have fun.

What troubled me the most was that he never received the help he needed. Thus he never recovered. And I never learned to know the real person—the happy, compassionate, and loving father—of whom I only caught glimpses once in a while.

My father's story may, at least in part, resemble your father's story, and his father's story, and now your story. And my own story may well have elements in common with your family's story. Many people have been traumatized by war and need to deal with the consequences. I could not help my father, but now I have a chance to help you and your family reintegrate and live your lives in a more positive way.

The reason I chose psychotherapy as my profession may well have been directly related to my father's history. In 1980 I graduated from the University of Maryland with a Master of Science degree in psychological counseling. I later became licensed and nationally certified. I have taught at two universities, conducted workshops nationally on several topics, and spoken on Post Traumatic Stress to both lay and professional groups.

I worked for a crisis counseling center and ran a large private practice for many years, specializing in counseling children, adults, and families who struggled with Post Traumatic Stress Disorder (PTSD). My clients included veterans and survivors of abuse, traumatic accidents, and natural disasters. Five days a week, I listened to seven or eight people per day who had experienced severe traumas. Underneath those often brave exteriors, I recognized the same types of pain for *all* people with PTSD. Although their experiences were varied and their traumas occurred in many different circumstances, the resulting physical and emotional symptoms were similar.

I have often wished that my clients and their families had understood how to deal with the traumas shortly after they happened. With proper treatment, perhaps their symptoms might have disappeared, or at least not worsened into severe disorders. Together, my clients and I worked to discover techniques that could help them recover. I give them a great deal of credit for many of the ideas shared in *How to Cope with Stress after Trauma*.

Whom is this book for?

Though this book is intended primarily for veterans, the strategies given are as valuable for anyone suffering from stress after *any* severe trauma, regardless of the cause. Psychotherapists and anyone working with survivors of severe trauma can use *How to Cope with Stress After Trauma* with their clients as an adjunct to therapy.

If you have picked up this book, you may be concerned there is something "wrong" with you or someone you love. If you are a veteran, you may be experiencing nightmares, sleeplessness, anxiety, and/or depression. You may have turned to addictive medications, illegal drugs, or alcohol for relief. You may feel agitated, or at times even become violent, reliving the terror of war, avoiding anything that triggers memories of traumatic events. Your hands may shake, or you may jump at unexpected noises or movements. If you or your loved one has any of these symptoms, this book is for you.[1]

---

[1] NOTE: This book is addressed to veterans who are experiencing Post Traumatic Stress (PTS), which is a milder condition with fewer stress symptoms than full-blown PTSD. However, I will refer to PTSD as well, because much more scientific research has been conducted on PTSD than on PTS. The other reason I refer frequently to PTSD is that the lesser stress symptoms of PTS may lead to a full-blown disorder if neglected for too long. That said, the strategies and steps offered here are intended for veterans who, although experiencing war-related stress, are still functional, and have not been diagnosed with PTSD. If you have been diagnosed with a "disorder," please seek counseling and medical help first and then add these steps to your recovery strategies where appropriate, and with your counselor's advisement.

Introduction

How to Cope with Stress After Trauma offers useful information and a recovery action plan geared toward veterans dealing with the trauma and stress caused by war who wish to cope with their problems before they worsen into a "disorder." It also offers help to families and friends who, nine times out of ten, are the people who make sure veterans get the help they need. These family members and friends desperately need to understand what is happening to their loved ones, and what they can do to help them.

According to a 2008 Rand Corporation study, about 20% of all veterans who have returned from Iraq and Afghanistan have been diagnosed with PTSD and, as a result, are no longer capable of leading what most of us would call "normal daily life." Their brains have malfunctioned due to excessive stress. The actual statistics may well be higher. Some veterans have chosen not to report their problems out of fear of negative repercussions, such as being stigmatized as weak and unfit for promotion or service.

At this point, let me debunk an old myth that has been believed for far too many years: People who experience a lot of stress following a trauma are weak. This myth is not true. The brain is an organ, just like any other organ in the body. When it malfunctions, certain symptoms arise. We don't consider people weak because they have had heart attacks, or because their lungs or kidneys have failed. Neither should we think of people as weak because their brains are not functioning normally.

Post Trauma Stress (PTS), as I use the term in this book, has similar but less severe symptoms than Post Traumatic Stress Disorder (PTSD). It affects many more veterans than does PTSD. Survivors with PTS remain functional, at least to some degree, and often have difficulty admitting that they somehow feel "different" than they did before joining the military. Family and friends usually notice these changes before the veteran does, as in the case of Josh.

Since returning from Iraq about two years ago, Josh has held five different jobs. Nightmares prevent him from sleeping more than a couple of hours a night. He becomes easily agitated and depressed, but the Veterans Administration (VA) does not consider his symptoms severe enough to be called PTSD. Recently his wife left with their two children, saying she couldn't handle his anger and inability to create a stable life for them. Like Josh, many veterans may be grappling with similar issues and problems every day, with little or no help.

And then there was Ellen who came to me after the first Iraq war. She had been a fighter pilot. When she called and I asked her what was going on she said she was afraid she was "going crazy." She would wake up in the middle of the night with nightmares of dropping bombs on the wrong targets and killing innocent children. Now she had panic attacks each morning when she sent her two girls off to school, afraid they would never return.

When a veteran comes home from the battlefield, loved ones with only the best intentions may expect him or her to forget the months or years spent in a war zone. They hope that if no one mentions it, life will return to normal. But that strategy didn't work for my father, the man of all strong men, many years ago, and it will most likely not work for you either.

Introduction

The steps in this book work. Many of my clients over the years have used them with great success. Although the verdict is still out on some of the newer technologies, I believe they are worth mentioning so you can explore them if you wish. But regardless of which strategies you decide to use, they all require an earnest and dedicated commitment to the healing process.

How to use this book

How to Cope with Stress *After Trauma* begins with a self-test to let you determine for yourself your current level of stress. Next I give you some basic information about Post Traumatic Stress (PTS) and Post Traumatic Stress Disorder (PTSD), such as symptoms to watch for. Then I offer several proven and effective strategies to stabilize and to deal with your pain, depression, and anxiety. The steps work somewhat like steps on a ladder. As you climb them one by one, they lead you closer and closer to your goal of recovery.

These steps and strategies form a comprehensive and detailed recovery program for everyone suffering from stress-related issues. I realize that you may feel overwhelmed when you look at all of them at once. Start by choosing only those that apply to you and fit with your lifestyle and beliefs. It may take a long time for you to complete a single step. That's okay. Sometimes slower is better.

If you feel unstable at this point, please start with Step One, which focuses on becoming stable. Then choose another step that you are willing to try, and so on. Some steps will work for you and some won't. Don't give up. Choose the ones that help you and practice them. There is a simple difference between those individuals who recover and those who don't: people who recover learn new ways to cope and dedicate their lives to using them.

Introduction

Our understanding of PTS is growing rapidly. The information I provide is current as of 2014. We live in an age of groundbreaking brain and memory research, and what is considered factual today may be superseded later by new information. I recommend you look online occasionally for the very latest data.

I wish I could grant you a quick solution to your problems, but I can't. The truth is that you will never be exactly the same as you were before you underwent a trauma. This is true of all human beings. Each memorable experience changes us. But it's also true that if you are willing to heal from the trauma, you may well change for the better. I have seen positive changes in attitude, inner peace, wisdom, and compassion develop in ways I would never have thought possible. Many of my former clients have gone on to help others with similar experiences and have changed individual lives and the greater world around them.

We, the people of the United States of America, have sent you to war and asked you to fight or even die for our freedom when necessary. Now it is time to act and help you, our veterans, regain healthy, happy, and productive lives at home. We will not abandon you now when you need us most. You have served us well. Now give us the chance to serve you.

You deserve to heal and prosper regardless of what you have experienced. If you feel a full recovery is too hard to commit to for yourself, please do it for your country and your loved ones. Even if you're not prepared to do all the steps involved in recovery, read this book anyway, and reread it when you are ready to make positive changes in your life.

You have already proven to our country that you are a positive force for change. And we are a grateful nation for your contribution to our freedom and security. Now it's time for you to take the next step and make that same contribution to yourself. You deserve it, and so do those around you whom you love.

It is not essential to read the entire book from beginning to end. Please check the table of contents and go to any step you may wish to use immediately.

Although I mention veteran's stories, I do not highlight traumatic details experienced by veterans in war. Instead I emphasize recovery after the trauma has occurred. All names of people in the book have been altered and stories are changed somewhat to assure the anonymity of my former clients.

The Healing Wall, Part I
by Patrick Overton, Ph.D. and Vietnam veteran

I.
I ignored the Wall –
for a long time.
I had managed to keep out unwanted reminders
of the memories of what I saw and did and felt
and the wall threatened to violate this self truce.
For a while I refused to go to the Wall.
I came close, but could not bring myself to go down
into that black hole –
So I stood there alone, on the perimeter
of the large descending block of large, cold stone,
and watched from the vantage point on the hill above.

Concealed by the autumn shadows,
hand pocketed, I turned my back and walked away,
mumbling to myself in a voice so low
even I couldn't hear what I was saying,
"Not today, I cannot do this today."

This passage is Part I of "The Healing Wall," written by a Vietnam veteran twenty years after his return to America. The poem appears in full at the end of the book.

Patrick Overton attended college on the GI bill, and later attended the University of Missouri where he earned his Ph.D. in Communication. He taught at Columbia College in Missouri for many years. "The Healing Wall" appears in his book, *Rebuilding the Front Porch of America*, published in 1997 and scheduled to be released again in 2015.

Before you continue, please take this test to determine your present stress level.

Post Traumatic Stress Test [2]

Place a number 1 to 5 in the blank next to each question according to how much you feel the statement applies to you:
  Number 1 is "not at all"
  Number 2 is "not often or not severe"
  Number 3 is "sometimes or moderate"
  Number 4 is "often or severe"
  Number 5 is "very often or very severe"

1. How frequently do you have recurring dreams or memories of the trauma? _____

2. How distressing are these memories? _____

3. How vividly do you remember the trauma in your memories and dreams? _____

---

[2] Note: Although there is a widely used assessment tool for PTSD called the Clinical Administrated PTSD Scale or CAPS, it is designed as a structured interview to be used by trained professionals. *The following is not a formal test and has not been researched for validity or reliability.* It is merely a short test I have created using the symptoms described in *The Diagnostic and Statistical Manual of Mental Health Disorders (DSM-IV)* to help you compare your levels of stress before the trauma and after. Please answer as honestly as you can. You may choose to share the results with someone else, or keep them private.

4. How often do you have flashbacks where you feel you are reliving the trauma? _____

5. How often do you feel like crying when you remember or speak about the trauma? _____

6. How often do you find yourself avoiding situations that trigger your memories of the trauma? _____

7. How severely do you think the trauma has affected you? _____

8. How often have your traumatic experiences or symptoms been ignored or belittled by others? _____

9. If you experienced trauma as a child, such as abuse, an accident, etc., how severe was it? _____
How often did it occur? _____

In this portion of the self-test, "Now" means "Today." "Before" means "Before experiencing combat (or other traumatic event)."

10. How often do you feel distant from other people, even your family? Now _____ Before _____

11. How often do you have problems falling or staying asleep? Now _____ Before _____

INTRODUCTION

12. How easily are you startled when something unexpected occurs? Now _____ Before _____

13. How often do you feel you are unable to function normally? Now _____ Before _____

14. How often are you on the lookout for threats or danger? Now _____ Before _____

15. How angry do you feel? Now _____ Before _____

16. How often do you have difficulty concentrating or feel confused? Now_____ Before _____

17. How often do you feel numb or have no feelings? Now _____ Before _____

18. How often do you experience outbursts of anger? Now_____ Before _____

19. How often are you depressed, anxious, or uninterested in things you used to enjoy? Now ____ Before _____

20. How often do you have symptoms such as a rapid heartbeat, shaking, perspiring, or tense muscles? Now ____ Before _____

21. How often do you think you may not live to be old? Now _____ Before_____

22. How often do you think about suicide?
    Now _____ Before_____

23. If you think about suicide, how detailed are your plans? _____

24. How often do you isolate yourself or spend time alone?
    Now_____ Before_____

25. How often are you ill or in pain? Now____Before ____

26. How often do you use alcohol or other drugs (legal or illegal) to help you cope with life? Now___ Before____

If most of your answers are marked 3 or under, you are probably a good candidate for the steps in this book. If your answers are mostly over 3, please seek professional help as soon as possible, and use this book in conjunction with more comprehensive therapy.

Where To Get Help

If you are thinking about or planning suicide, contact the VA suicide hotline at 1-800-273-8255, your doctor, or 911 immediately.

Chat: www.veteranscrisisline.net
Text: 838255

The veteran's hotline, chat, and text now have more than 300 trained staff to assist you.

If you are a veteran suffering from PTSD or severe stress after the trauma of war, call your local VA hospital or Veteran's Center (Vet Center) for help. Vet Centers offer free counseling to combat veterans and their families.

For more information about the services available for you, call the VA Health Benefits Service Center at 1-877-222-VETS or call your local VA, Vet Center, community volunteer programs or church.

For help locating a trauma therapist, treatment center, or support group in your area, contact the Sidran Traumatic Stress Institute at 1-410-825-8888, ext. 203

Also check the Internet and the Wounded Warrior Project.

There is help for you.

PART ONE

Information about stress after a trauma, often called Post Traumatic Stress (PTS) and Post Traumatic Stress Disorder (PTSD)

Accurate information is essential to healing.

Note: You can read this section now, or turn immediately to the steps you need, then return to this information later.

What Are Post Traumatic Stress (PTS) and Post Traumatic Stress Disorder (PTSD)?

Years ago, as a psychotherapist working in private practice, I earned a reputation in my community for my work with people who dealt with severe trauma. Social service agencies often referred clients to me, sometimes from as far as two hundred miles away.

A husky, muscular man I'll call Joe, then in his mid-thirties, came to me via the Veterans Administration (VA). About ten years earlier, Joe had completed a tour of duty in Vietnam, and since then he had survived without help, although he reluctantly admitted to having problems sleeping and nightmares about his combat experience.

Joe had been employed at a sawmill for several years and he loved his work. Recently, however, the owner of the adjoining property had opened a gun range. Soon after, Joe developed a phobia to what he called "loud noise." Every time he heard a shot, he jumped, covered his head, and crouched behind a pile of logs. His heart raced, and he shook for several minutes.

Understandably, he decided to change jobs.

He expected his phobia to end, but instead, whenever a car backfired or he heard a loud bang, he reacted in a similar way as he had to the gunshots. Over the previous couple of months he had spent much of his time trying to avoid people and loud noises. He couldn't work. He had frequent nightmares and woke up sweating. Having slept very little, he had become unpredictably explosive toward his wife and children. She was threatening to take the children and leave if the problem didn't stop. In plain words, his life had become unmanageable.

When Joe arrived in my office, I noticed his face was drawn and his hands trembled. The first words he said to me after explaining his symptoms were, "This has nothing to do with Vietnam."

I took a deep breath, nodded, and said, "Then let's find out what's really going on."

I asked him to tell me his family history, starting with his childhood. He told me that his father was an alcoholic and that life at home had been difficult. Within less than five minutes, however, he switched from stories about his childhood to stories about his experiences on the front line in Vietnam. His memories were so vivid, it was as though they had happened yesterday.

In time, Joe dealt with his symptoms, and eventually with his memories. During our year together, Joe did not forget his two years in Vietnam: the hand-to-hand combat, the many men in his platoon who died, the women and children he thought he could trust but who carried weapons, the innocent people he killed in the villages. Most of all, he never forgot the guilt and shame he felt when he came home.

(Like many who served in Vietnam, instead of receiving a hero's welcome, he was shunned or ignored by his countrymen.) Yes, the memories were still there, but they were much less intense. They no longer triggered flashbacks and nightmares. Joe's anger subsided, and after a short separation from his family, he returned home.

Why did I start the book with Joe's story? Because I think it's a familiar story to veterans. Regardless of which war you fought—World War II, the Korean War, the Vietnam War, Operation Just Cause in Panama, the Gulf War, Operation Iraqi Freedom, Operation Enduring Freedom in Afghanistan, or any other war—the lessons learned will be similar.

THE FIRST LESSON:
Don't make excuses or ignore your first symptoms of Post Traumatic Stress. The sooner you deal with the symptoms, the more likely they will recede into the past without your becoming dysfunctional or developing what psychologists call a "disorder."

THE SECOND LESSON:
Although most Post Traumatic Stress occurs in the immediate aftermath of a trauma, delayed reactions are common. Months or years may pass before they manifest in the conscious mind. Usually there is a trigger event that sets off the symptoms. For Joe, this event was the sound of gunshots from the range next door to his workplace.

THE THIRD LESSON:
You are strong, not weak, when you face life and deal with it as it happens instead of pretending there's nothing wrong. It is a sign of strength to ask for help. Anyone—and I mean anyone—may have a reaction to trauma similar to Joe's. I hope that some of the steps in this book will help you learn how to cope, but if they don't relieve your symptoms, see a psychotherapist and/or a medical doctor.

THE FOURTH LESSON:
You are not alone, even though you may feel as if you are. Certainly combat veterans are unique to some extent, regarding the specifics of their trauma. It is very important for you to meet with other veterans, who can understand you in a way civilians at home can't. But regardless of who people are or the type of severe trauma they have been exposed to—whether it occurred in war, in an accident, in a natural disaster, or in an abusive situation— all are human beings. As humans, our bodies and brains control our emotions and minds and tend to respond to trauma in similar ways. Some react more severely, some less so, for a longer or shorter time, but millions around the globe experience trauma symptoms that are similar. However, people in varying cultures may respond and answer questions about trauma symptoms somewhat differently, depending on their priorities.

THE FIFTH LESSON:
Recovery is possible. If you get help, your symptoms will most likely lessen to the point where they can be easily managed.

Although PTS and PTSD are much more complex than can be addressed here, I hope that this book will give you a basic understanding of what is happening in your body, mind, and emotions. I have deliberately attempted to avoid discussing anything that might trigger your traumatic memories, but if at any time you feel overwhelmed or flooded by emotions as you read, make sure that you stop reading, take some deep breaths, and do something that you love to do and that helps you relax. For many veterans, physical exercise of any kind helps. Even those who have been injured can usually work out in some way to exercise. In addition, or if physical exercise doesn't seem to help, then read Step One on stabilizing and follow its recommendations.

Information is power and gives you back some of the control you felt you lost during and after the trauma. Most people don't know much about PTS or PTSD, but the sooner you know the facts, the sooner recovery will begin.

Research suggests that there are **three factors that consistently lead to stress: uncertainty, lack of information, and loss of control.** As you learn, you'll find your stress reactions reducing. So when you feel ready, continue reading Part One and any other information that you trust. Personal accounts of recovery from other veterans can be very helpful, especially if you identify with them, but make sure you remember that everyone is different and reacts somewhat differently. What worked for one person may not help you, just as some of the steps I provide may not work for you. Try them and find the best ones. Then practice them daily.

If you read articles that make exaggerated claims of instant, complete recovery, be careful of the writer's information and suggested techniques. Although I imagine instant recoveries do occur, they are rare. For most people, recovery is a process that takes time— weeks, months, and sometimes years. But by then the symptoms have receded to such an extent that life is manageable again.

A Definition of
PTS and PTSD

Severe stress is a normal bodily response to an unusual and difficult traumatic experience. Often the trauma is perceived as life-threatening to you or the people you love. Symptoms occur most frequently after a traumatic event that happens suddenly, repeatedly, or over a long period of time, such as in war. The trauma triggers the body's survival mechanism, called the "freeze, fight, or flight" response. A normal reaction to a severe stressor usually includes shock, intense fear, anxiety, numbness, and depression.

The body has an amazing ability to keep you functioning during a crisis, but in the aftermath of the trauma, when the adrenaline and other stress hormones stop flowing, some people may collapse or become non-functional. Others have symptoms of trauma but may continue to function. Still others may not experience symptoms until years after the triggering trauma.

Simply stated, the way I define the terms in this book, Post Traumatic Stress (PTS) is Post Traumatic Stress Disorder (PTSD) without the "Disorder." Where do people draw the line between the two? As with most things in life, you will find considerable controversy on the topic, particularly in the military, as more and more armed services personnel are reporting symptoms while overseas, and even more after discharge.

With PTS, although bad memories and physical symptoms interfere with a person's everyday life, he or she remains functional enough to continue working and, at least to some degree, fulfill his or her role as a soldier, spouse, parent, friend, employee, and family and community member. Usually severe physical and emotional symptoms last for less than a month after a major stressful event, and the body and emotions automatically normalize to a point where the person can once again function. However, he or she may spend a great deal of energy doing so.

PTSD is a more severe condition than PTS. PTSD sufferers' symptoms are prolonged and severe. They can no longer keep a job, continue normal relationships with family and friends, or function in society on a day-to-day basis.

PTS symptoms, if not addressed promptly following a trauma, may develop into PTSD. On the other hand, immediate treatment of PTS symptoms, like most preventative programs, might well save you from the torture and heartache of PTSD.

The following two case studies of Vietnam veterans illustrate the far-reaching effects of PTSD:

After completing his tour of duty, Richard became an alcoholic. In spite of losing his family and his job, he did not seek help until he almost shot someone during a flashback and was court-ordered to seek counseling. He struggled for years and eventually turned his life around with the help of medications, Alcoholics Anonymous, group meetings at the

VA, and his church. Forty years later, he is finally symptom-free and no longer needs prescription drugs to remain functional.

Michael spent his tour of duty slogging through miles of rice fields and swamps, tracking down the Vietcong. He was in constant pain due to several pieces of shrapnel in one leg. After returning from Vietnam in 1973, he studied to become a social worker, then got a job working in the probation system in Utah. However, he was only able to work for a few years before his war memories and reactions became so severe that he was finally placed on disability.

Except for sleep medication, anxiety-reducing drugs, and painkillers, he refused treatment, too proud to admit he needed psychotherapy. Meanwhile, his symptoms continued to escalate. When he went out to eat, or even to a friend's house, he refused to sit near a window or with his back to the door, always on alert. He isolated himself, drank heavily, then added more prescription drugs, mostly painkillers. He experienced outbursts of rage, one time nearly shooting his wife. After she died of cancer, he isolated himself entirely. Not long ago, he attempted suicide. He now lives in a veterans' home, unable to care for himself. Unlike Richard, by not seeking help for PTSD, he never regained a normal life.

Would immediate treatment of PTS symptoms have lessened Richard's and Michael's symptoms and therefore changed their lives? Research now indicates that it might well have helped. I wish we could have given them a chance to chose a different path soon after their traumas occurred. Both served in the front lines during the Vietnam War. Both experienced PTS as a result. Neither received immediate treatment when they returned home, and both developed severe PTSD several years later and were placed on disability. Only Richard eventually made a full recovery.

Milder PTS symptoms generally decrease soon after the trauma and gradually disappear. However, through no fault of yours, you may get stuck in the "on" position or be triggered again later. Maybe this metaphor will help you understand what happens when your body gets trapped in trauma mode. Picture the doorbell on your front door. You hear the doorbell ring and go to the door, but nobody is there. You expect the bell to stop, but it keeps on ringing. By now it's obvious the bell is stuck. You try to stop it, but it just keeps ringing. You try to ignore it as long as you can, but your family and neighbors are staring at you. Some even call out, "Can't you do something about that doorbell?"

You dash to your toolbox, grab a toolkit, and dash back to your door. You try to repair the bell, but you don't know how. Frustrated, angry, and agitated at the constant noise in your head, you might even hit the bell with a hammer. Now you have a broken doorbell, probably even a broken door, but the bell still keeps ringing. Why did **your** doorbell get stuck and not your neighbor's? Who knows? Stuff happens. But now your only options are to let the doorbell keep on ringing, or to accept that it's broken and find a skilled repairman to fix it.

Where does the diagnosis of PTSD originate?

Whenever we hear the term PTSD in the media, it is usually associated with combat troops in war, rarely with accidents, abuse, or natural disasters. And to some degree, the reporters are right. During World War I, the U. S. military first recognized the cluster of symptoms now called PTSD. Back then the disorder was called "shell shock." After World War II, it became known as "combat stress disorder" or "combat fatigue."

As time went on, researchers and psychologists realized that *any* person might respond to sudden, severe, and unusual stress in a way similar to soldiers in battle. The condition became known as Post Traumatic Stress Disorder, and in 1980 was added to the American handbook used to diagnose psychological problems, *The Diagnostic Statistical Manual, Third Edition* (*DSM-III*), in the "Anxiety Disorders" category. In the most recently released edition, *DSM-V*, PTSD is listed under a new category, "Trauma and Stressor Related Disorders."

What types of trauma can cause severe stress?

Here is a list of the types of trauma that cause PTS or PTSD, although all of these will likely not pertain to you directly:

- Experiencing or witnessing **a natural disaster,** including diseases, earthquakes, forest fires, hurricanes, tornadoes, tsunamis, and severe flooding, such as has taken place recently in New Orleans, New York, and Boulder, Colorado. Most of us think of these natural disasters as acts of God, entirely out of our control.

- Experiencing or witnessing **an accident,** such as a serious car accident, plane crash, house fire, or collapse of a building. We think of these as manmade disasters. However, most of us can understand that accidents are part of life and no one meant them to happen.

- Experiencing or witnessing **a premeditated tragedy.** This category includes murders, child abuse, sexual and physical assaults, school shootings, kidnappings, torture, bombings, war, and terrorist attacks, like the one many of us remember that took place on September 11, 2001.

Take a guess as to which of the three types of trauma tend to create symptoms of PTS and PTSD most frequently and severely. If you guessed premeditated disasters, you are correct. Actually the answer is quite logical. Nature has normal cycles of storms, disease, and earth movements. Accidents happen. But most of us can find few excuses for people who have deliberately killed or injured someone else, except in self-defense. In a premeditated tragedy, your loved one's death or your own injuries were intentionally inflicted and could have been prevented.

I believe there is a fourth category often ignored, though more frequently mentioned today than in the past:

- **Secondary PTS:** This condition affects people who did not actually experience or witness the trauma in person, including military personnel not directly engaged in battle, first responders, clinicians who work with PTSD survivors, and police officers who must report a death to loved ones. They see the results of the trauma—the blood and suffering—even though they didn't experience it firsthand. Another group of secondary PTS sufferers, often overlooked, are the loved ones of those who have PTS or PTSD, such as family and friends who can only imagine the trauma. The human mind is very powerful and may well be able to construct mental images of traumas so vivid that they affect our emotions and bodies.

Let's take war as an example. Since the media is saturated with graphic depictions of war and violence, it is fairly easy for civilians to imagine in excruciating detail what combat is like for soldiers: the constant danger, the improvised explosive devices (IEDs), the bombs exploding nearby, loved ones suffering injuries, the sounds and smells of the battlefield. These images can indirectly trigger secondary PTS.

In recent wars, Skype has allowed military personnel to see and talk to their families or partners while stationed overseas. What an incredible invention! In the great majority of these communications, your loved ones will be much relieved to know you're okay. But very occasionally, actually seeing you in uniform and in a combat zone or dangerous area may be an indirect trigger for them to imagine the worst and react with PTS symptoms.

What Qualifies as an Unusual and/or Severe Trauma?

The *Diagnostic Statistical Manual* (*DSM-IV*) defines severe and unusual trauma as an incident outside the realm of ordinary human experiences such as simple bereavement, chronic illness, family conflict, or economic loss. Of course, many of the symptoms of PTS can occur with these "usual" traumas as well, and the steps to recovery that follow are just as helpful to those people. Regardless of how other people classify an event, ultimately the trauma is severe and unusual if **you** perceive it that way.

However, the stressors I am talking about in this book are usually sudden and cause intense fear, terror, and helplessness; a total loss of control; powerlessness; and a feeling that there is no safe place.

In war, such situations include a threat to your life, a threat to your body, or a threat to the people in your unit. Too often the experience results in the loss of a limb or normal body function, or the death of a friend or of several platoon members whom you think of as brothers or sisters. Sometimes you are the first responder to a gruesome scene, such as an incident with an IED.

Is it any wonder that many people will do almost anything —including becoming violent, avoiding reminders of the trauma, and denying they have a problem—in order to regain feelings of control and safety? To regain a sense of control, veterans may respond by withdrawing or becoming angry and aggressive. These responses are prompted by fear—a perfectly understandable emotion, but which nonetheless needs to be addressed. Ask yourself, "What am I afraid of?" The answer will assist you in finding a solution to your individual situation.

The greater the number of the five senses involved in the incident, the more powerful the effects. Although we often remember sights and sounds, we tend to forget that smell, taste, and touch can be just as powerful and multiply the impact of an event. For example, the scent of roses may mentally transport a person back to a mother's funeral. A man who worked in the vicinity of the Twin Towers when the planes crashed into them on September 11, 2001, remembers seeing the fireball and hearing the terrifying explosion. He also remembers the acrid smell of the smoke and the taste and feel of grit in his mouth. Interestingly, it was the feeling of grit in his mouth that most caused him to relive the events of 9/11 in his mind.

In the course of my work, I noticed that much of the seriousness and severity of a trauma depended on the person's own **perception** of what occurred. So think for a minute. What were you taught as a child? About life? About war? What have your religion and culture taught you? How significant was the event to you? For some, the trauma may have mirrored events from your past that you thought were severe, even though others might not have seen the event in the same way. Only you can define for yourself whether a trauma was severe or not, and to what degree.

A military officer who served in Afghanistan told me a story of finding the body of a young boy blown apart by an IED. With a heavy heart, the officer wrapped the body, knelt down, said a prayer, saluted, and buried the boy. Another soldier who experienced the same event reacted very little. Why the difference? The first officer thought it might be because he was married and had a little boy about the same age as the dead child. He understood what it would be like to lose a child. The other soldier, a nineteen-year-old, had no similar attachments.

If something important to you is suddenly lost, or if you believe something exists but then it is gone, you may feel intense fear, insecurity, vulnerability, and grief. This is what happened to many Americans after the terrorist attacks on the World Trade Center. Up to that time, we had felt safe in the United States, as if no one from outside could harm us. We were in control. But when the terrorists blew up the Twin Towers, suddenly our sense of security was shattered. Our security had been an illusion, but our belief that we were safe had kept us from feeling fear. When that belief disappeared, we clung to our government to make us feel safe again, even though that was impossible. I don't know for sure, but I imagine that people living in countries such as Ireland and Israel, where terrorist attacks are frequent, might have perceived the event differently because they have always known they were susceptible to sudden attacks.

Are Some People More Vulnerable to Stress After a Trauma Than Others?

Although everyone is vulnerable to stress and susceptible to PTS, some people are more prone to it than others. Why? Mostly because of their genes. That's not their fault, and it isn't anything they can change.

Why do some people experience more severe stress reactions than others? While some people do not seem to be affected by prolonged stress after a trauma and return to feeling normal shortly after the stressors abate, depending on the situation and your particular inherited nervous system and brain, you may be more susceptible to stress.

Interestingly, researchers have found that people who have been genetically gifted with the strongest memories are also more vulnerable to PTSD. A recent study by a neuroscientist at the University of Basel, Switzerland, discovered some people have a genetic signature that gives them the ability to form stronger memories. After studying 347 refugees of the Rwandan genocide, researchers found a clear indication that stronger memories were linked to a heightened risk of PTSD, often doubling the risk.

Recent research also indicates that women are more prone than men to develop PTSD, possibly twice as often. Why? At this point we don't know, although functional MRI studies by Daniel Amen have shown that female brains function differently from men's brains in certain respects. Also, a woman's social and cultural environment differs from a man's. So it would not be surprising that men and women might react differently to stress as well.

The strength and severity of PTSD is also linked to genetic causes. If you have any genetically transmitted mental disorder, such as bipolar disorder, schizophrenia, or inherited depression, it can reduce your ability to deal with stress. Although gene variations for stress vulnerability are primarily inherited at conception, researchers are now finding that environmental factors, especially when experienced early in life, can create changes in the body that permanently alter your susceptibility to stress. Thus childhood trauma and/or abuse may have a lasting effect not only on the mind, but also on the DNA.

A study conducted at McGill University in Quebec revealed DNA modifications that made people who were physically and/or sexually abused as children more sensitive to severe stress as they grew up. In certain people, the number of cortical hormone (stress hormone) receptors had actually been reduced. Although the research subjects were studied for abuse only, it is likely that any child growing up under prolonged, severe stress, such as in an alcoholic or violent family or neighborhood, or with a parent suffering from an emotional disorder, may experience similar changes in how he or she reacts to stress as an adult.

Biochemistry also plays a part. Researchers have found that the fetal stress response of a child in the womb is a biochemical reflection of the mother's stress condition. As a result, children subjected to stress in the womb bear a biochemical tendency to react more strongly to stress in the future.

Learning is another important factor in stress susceptibility. As I have mentioned, certain beliefs and values you were taught in the past may affect your perceptions of what happens to you in the present.

If you perceive you are more susceptible to stress than the people around you, remember, you are not at fault. And you are not alone. There are many, many people who may have these same vulnerabilities. Don't give up. Be cautious with medication, but don't rule it out. These are physical disorders that often can be successfully treated with a balancing chemical, the way insulin balances diabetes.

From my readings and experience of working with people who have PTSD, I've learned that the longer, more severe, or more continuous the stress, or the more frequently it occurs (such as in war), the more likely it will become unmanageable. The person never feels safe, and the mind and body can take only so much stress before they malfunction. Once the person believes he or she is in control over his or her life, the stress fades.

Prolonged stress can lead to the dysregulation of the sympathetic nervous system, which governs bodily functions not under our conscious control (like breathing). If a person is experiencing a constant state of arousal, the nervous system can get stuck in the "on" state. As I mentioned earlier, I compare it to a stuck doorbell or a stuck horn on your car. The doorbell and the horn have very useful purposes, but they become irritating and disruptive if they won't stop. Just so, the "freeze, fight, or flight" response is essential to alert us to and help us escape from danger, but it becomes dysfunctional if it won't stop after the threat is gone. When this system does not recalibrate to a normal level after the threat stops, PTS or PTSD can occur and the person begins to experience symptoms such as restlessness, nightmares, hyper-vigilance, muscle pain, and headaches.

Research has found that military personnel are predisposed to developing PTSD as a result of their training. Military training is generally geared to shutting down or cutting off thoughts and emotions in a time of crisis. If you are a veteran, you have been taught to react instantaneously when you perceive danger, instead of thinking and then acting. You have been trained to follow a command. You must flip into survival mode and shoot in order to save yourself and others. While this automatic reaction is necessary in combat, it makes life a lot more difficult after you come home. It is not easy to erase your training and relearn to take a moment of thought before you respond to a situation. In the next section I will tell you about a veteran who is now serving a twenty-five year prison term because of this problem.

Other studies indicate that a lack of understanding from others plays a role in the increased likelihood of developing PTS or PTSD. This lack may take the form of people accusing you of feigning your symptoms or failing to understand what you are going through. Perhaps they believe in the old school of "hard knocks" and say or imply that your war trauma is not severe, or is simply a case of bad nerves. They may advise you to "just buck up and get over it." The more people in your life who downplay or disrespect your experiences, the greater your stress and the more severe your PTS reaction.

In a particularly sad example, some Vietnam veterans (like Joe, whose story I told earlier) came home to members of the public who despised and shamed them for their actions in the service of their country. Certainly this disheartening public reaction may have greatly increased the likelihood of PTSD in some Vietnam veterans. But you may experience a lack of support just as easily from members of your own family or community, no matter which war you fought.

So, yes, there are people who are more vulnerable to stress than others, but if you are one of them, the steps in Part Two can help you. You can't control your genetics or your past, but you can **learn** ways of coping with situations that will lessen their impact considerably and help you return to normal functioning. When you use these strategies, you will be able to change your stress level at any time you wish. Eventually you will feel back in control of your mind, emotions, and body, and your symptoms of stress will decrease.

How prevalent are
PTS and PTSD?

Though statistics are not always as precise or accurate as we might like, and may vary from one study to another, nonetheless they offer an overall picture of a trend or situation. Following are the most up-to-date and reliable statistics I found concerning PTS and PTSD.

According to the United States Department of Veterans Affairs, between 7% and 8% of the U.S. population will experience PTSD some time in their lives. About ten years after the Vietnam War ended, the most rigorous study indicated that about 30.9% of troops had suffered from PTSD, and 15% were still suffering at the time of the study. Many more troops had experienced Post Trauma Stress (PTS) as I have defined it.

While statistics have not yet been fully tabulated for the Iraq and Afghanistan wars, they are projected to be similar to those reported for past wars. Some studies, such as the 2008 Rand Corporation study, place the percentage of veterans from these wars who have experienced PTSD and/or major depression at about 20%. An article on the Disabled American Veterans website estimates a percentage closer to one-third, with a third of all spouses and children of veterans having experienced emotional problems as well.

Recent random-sample studies of veterans performed by the U. S. military found rates of PTSD much lower than previously expected. The most rigorous study, the U. S. Millennium Cohort, indicated rates of PTSD as low as 7.6% for combatants, although one part of the same study found about 20%.

The veterans studied had been randomly selected from among soldiers who did not exhibit symptoms of PTSD prior to combat, thus eliminating veterans whose symptoms predated the war. As both a psychotherapist and a citizen of this country who cares about its veterans, these results raise questions in my mind, as they probably do in yours. What about the veterans who develop PTSD as many as eight or ten years after serving in combat? As we've seen, many people, through no fault of their own, are more vulnerable to PTSD than others. By eliminating soldiers who exhibited some symptoms of PTSD at the time of enlistment, the study was unable to measure how much their symptoms worsened during the war. Obviously these soldiers must have been functional at the time of enlistment, or the military would not have accepted them, especially for a combat mission. At worst they must have had what I call PTS. And are we to leave these many veterans without assistance because the military does not want to include them among the veterans who have PTSD purely as a result of the war?

It is estimated that only half of veterans who need help actually get it because of their dread of being labeled "mentally ill." They fear being seen as weak, especially if the stigma of mental illness presents a threat to advancement or possibility of dismissal. In 2005 Marine Major John Ruocco hanged himself between Iraq deployments. His wife said he had been unable to bring himself to seek help because of his fear of how others would see him. He thought the military would think he was weak or trying to get out of redeploying or serving his country. In reality, Major Ruocco suffered from untreated depression. It is time for us to let go of these old beliefs that depressed people and those with PTS or PTSD are weak or shirking their duty, and understand what can happen in the brain under severe stress and trauma.

According to a recent study, five times as many divorces occur among veterans than other couples. Jeremy, a twenty-four-year old Afghanistan veteran with PTSD, told me that out of five friends who had returned from the war, he was the only one not divorced. He attributed his intact marriage to the patience and caring of his spouse. She had gone online to educate herself about PTSD and understood what was happening to him.

Did you know that about 90% of soldiers survived their physical injuries in the last Iraq and Afghanistan war? Compared to earlier wars, this is incredible. Medicine has come a long distance. But this survival rate also means that many veterans must live with severe physical injuries. They may have lost limbs, or eyes, or hearing. And one in five veterans has Traumatic Brain Injury (TBI), a condition often accompanied by PTSD.

Some estimates claim that, at any one time, at least 260,000 veterans are homeless, and about 40,000 veterans a year are released from prisons without counseling. Most of these incarcerations result from drug abuse and violence.

A 2008 study reported on Medscape found that PTSD and alcoholism are closely linked, as troops turn to alcohol to cope with their problems and severe stress. 63% of the Reserve and National Guard soldiers studied were more likely to start drinking heavily, and 23% began to binge-drink after deployment. Younger troops were most at risk. I imagine the statistics might be similar with other drugs.

In recent years more soldiers and veterans have died of suicide than are killed in battle. According to *Army News*, each day eighteen veterans (of all wars) succeed in ending their lives, and about one active duty soldier a day commits suicide. The statistics for 2010 suggested that twenty-two veterans per day ended their own lives. (It is important to note, however, that the suicide rate for American citizens as a whole has also increased over this time period.)

When Bruce, a young man who lived in our neighborhood, arrived home from Iraq after three tours of duty, his family said they hardly knew him. He was withdrawn and often stared into space. "He wasn't inside there," his mother said. At times he would suddenly rage and throw things at his wife, who became afraid for her life and left, taking their four-year-old daughter with her.

After that, the only people Bruce spent time with were other veterans, whom he felt understood him. Only months after he arrived home, he and a couple of his army buddies got drunk and played Russian roulette using the weapon Bruce always carried. As you have probably guessed, Bruce died in the "game."

I imagine the military wanted to protect the family by labeling the death a "weapons accident." That's understandable, but in the meantime, by not acknowledging a suicide situation for what it really is, they have done no service to the military personnel and their families who desperately need help and are not receiving it. People don't point a loaded gun at their head and pull the trigger unless they are consciously or unconsciously willing to die. Not even when they are drinking. Probably all the men in the group were suicidal, although only one died. I sincerely hope that the others have received help.

Why is the present suicide rate among veterans so high? According to the military, the reasons for the increase are not fully known. It may be due to better tracking of statistics, misuse of prescription drugs, feelings of alienation, and/or difficulty readjusting to family and civilian life after multiple combat tours. Many troops say they have lost their purpose in life when they return and feel they are wasting their time. Others feel alone, missing the camaraderie of others in their unit who understood them. They feel no one at home understands them, not even their spouses and children or former best friends. Some suffer from survivor guilt after seeing fellow soldiers killed without being able to help them. And some have lost all faith in a loving God, or any sense that their lives can change for the better. As if that's not bad enough, as we have seen, many avoid treatment because of the stigma associated with mental illness.

In 2012, with the Iraq war ended and the war in Afghanistan drawing to a close, suicide rates escalated among active military, even among soldiers who had never seen combat. About 31% of military suicides involved troops who had never been deployed to a war zone. But in 2013, after the military put several new preventive programs into place, the rate dropped by 22%.

Although PTSD is one cause of suicide, obviously there are others as well. Many veterans are depressed, hopeless, and anxious. They fear an insecure, unknown future in a country where the jobless rate is high and social services are being cut. Many have personal financial problems and feel they have no control over what will happen next. The Veteran's Administration can take months, sometimes more than a year, before processing disability claims. Meanwhile, veterans are left without financial or medical help.

In my experience of working with suicidal clients, few of them actually want to die. Most of them desperately want their physical, mental, and emotional pain to stop, and they can see no other solution except to end their lives. It is sad to hear that there are still senior army generals such as Major General Dana Pittard, who blogged that suicide is an "absolutely selfish act" and admonished the men to "be an adult and act like an adult." I sincerely hope that he will never have to deal with so much pain and hopelessness that he feels that there is no other way out. Instead of berating depressed soldiers let's find ways to help them.

Over the years, I have wondered why the families of veterans who killed themselves were not sent a condolence letter from the President, as with other military deaths. Now, finally, that neglect is being reversed and the President is sending condolences to the families of suicide victims in the military. Has our attitude toward suicide finally changed? I hope so. In my view, those soldiers have given as much to their country as any others. They have given not only their bodies, but also their emotions, and their minds.

The problems are urgent. But please remember, many answers are available now to assist you through this time and help you readjust back into civilian life. Working together, we can find solutions. Family members and friends, did you know that according to the VA, about 9 out of 10 veterans who seek help for psychological issues are pressured to come by you? And that many of the veterans who eventually recover, do so because of your love and understanding? Thank you. Although counseling is not always the answer, it is one of the best ways you or a loved one can start on the road to recovery.

Veterans and families, it is time to take charge of your lives again.

What are the symptoms of PTS and PTSD?

PTS affects the body, emotions, mind, and spiritual life. Veterans, now that you are home, are you having problems sleeping? Do you jump at noise? Are you hyper vigilant, watching for trouble? Depressed and anxious? Maybe harboring unacknowledged thoughts of suicide? Do you relive the war during nightmares or flashbacks? Are you easily agitated, argumentative, or explosive with your mate or children? Do you isolate yourself? Are you using drugs and/or alcohol to cover your feelings and pain? **Even if you have only some of these symptoms, you may have PTS. Depending on how severe your symptoms are, you may well have the more severe PTSD.**

In my practice I prefer to look at each person as an individual with unique issues, but for this situation I have used a symptom list as compiled by the *DSM-IV*. The list is used by therapists to determine whether a person suffers from PTSD. Symptoms of PTS would be milder. For example, a PTS sufferer will probably not have flashbacks, though he or she may well have nightmares and sometimes vivid memories, but not as frequently as with PTSD.

Millions of people around the world suffer with severe stress after a trauma. Symptoms are similar for everyone but the center of attention can be different. Although we in the western world tend to focus most on the psychological symptoms, some other cultures focus most on the physical symptoms such as muscle aches, headaches, and illnesses, and on the social disruption that the trauma has caused.

IN PTSD, THE TRAUMATIZED PERSON:

1. Has memories, flashbacks, or nightmares of the event. You may actually feel you are reliving the war trauma, or you may have intrusive recollections of the war through sudden memories and dreams. For many, the event seems real at that moment, and they literally believe they are back in the experience.

Robert, a powerful warrior honored for his bravery in Vietnam and Panama, felt life was meaningless and boring when he returned home. In order to feel useful and excited about life again, he joined the police force.

One night about eight years after he left the Marines, he was sent on a drug raid with his partner and a couple of other policemen. Before they knew what was happening, one of the criminals held a gun to Robert's partner's head. Robert lunged for the man. Just that quickly, he was mentally back in Vietnam. The first thing he remembered were other police officers shouting at him to stop. When he came back to reality, he saw he had shoved a gun into the drug dealer's throat and almost shot him. Robert left the police force soon after the incident. Although this was the first flashback he had experienced since combat, he was afraid it might happen again. The flashbacks continued for years, but after therapy, Robert is doing well.

2. Has intense bodily fear reactions (racing heart, tensed muscles, shaking, nausea, sweating, indigestion, etc.) Heart arrhythmias are so common among veterans that, in the past, they were called "soldier's heart." Many soldiers were afraid they were having heart attacks. These physical symptoms can occur when a person with PTS is exposed to an event that triggers memories of the trauma, or even some small aspect of it. The stimulus or trigger places the person back into the trauma. Even the anniversary of an event can re-traumatize a person. Many veterans who viewed the movie *Saving Private Ryan* experienced flashbacks and nightmares.

3. Deliberately evades trigger(s) and numbs out or dissociates to avoid emotional pain. PTSD sufferers attempt to avoid places, thoughts, feelings, and situations that remind them of the trauma, or trigger flashbacks. Joe, introduced in Part One, stopped working, then hid in his house so he would not hear the sounds that took him mentally back to Vietnam. Other war veterans have moved to the mountains or into the forest, away from civilization, to try to evade the things that will trigger flashbacks. Sometimes people feel detached from others and are no longer interested in life or in the things they enjoyed previously. Some feel numb, with little ability to feel emotions such as intimacy or tenderness. For others, even anger is absent. Many of these veterans feel depressed and have a very limited sense of the future. My father, who lived with PTS most of his life, frequently said, "I won't live that long." He lived to be eighty-eight.

4. Has sleeping problems. People with PTSD experience increased arousal and anxiety that make it difficult for them to relax and fall or stay asleep. These people are constantly on "red alert" and overly watchful. A person with PTS feels jumpy, is easily startled, and feels as if he or she is in imminent danger. Although some think of these symptoms as a sleep disorder, many doctors now look at them as an anxiety disorder.

5. Can have difficulty concentrating or finishing what he or she started. This perceived lack of follow-through creates problems in relationships, work, and school. One of my clients said that he felt as if his mind was in a fog, always split in pieces, some in the present and some in the past. Even though he tried, he could never get rid of the fog long enough to find all the pieces and put them back together.

6. May have minutes of lost memories, or details of certain parts of the memories that cannot be retrieved. Veterans may even forget important parts of the incident. When Carl's jeep hit an IED on the way to Fallujah, he was tossed many feet into the air and landed on some rocks. He was diagnosed with Traumatic Brain Injury and later with PTSD. When I asked him what had happened, he said he remembered nothing between the explosion and his arrival at the hospital. The soldier driving the jeep behind him, however, said Carl had remained conscious throughout the entire process. The loss of memory might be due to the brain injury, but it might also be due to Carl's mind not wanting to remember.

Researchers at the University of Colorado at Boulder are now saying that they may soon be able to explain the techniques that the brain uses to wipe out unwanted memories, like severe traumas. What they are discovering is that the conscious mind can literally say "no" to remembering certain events after they happen. Is this the brain's incredible way of protecting us from traumatic memories we cannot deal with at that time? Whether these memories can be retrieved later is still not known.

7. May become irritable when he or she fears loss of control of a situation or person, or may actually become aggressive with unpredictable explosions of rage. Remember that rage comes from fear, especially fear of your life being out of your control. Everything is uncertain and you feel your life depends on you getting back some power to be able to feel safe and sane again. I think this fear of loss of control is the major issue for humanity. Whenever you are afraid, ask yourself, "What am I afraid of losing?" The answer is usually, "Loss of power and control." You think, "I can't control what others do, say, or think, or what will happen to me next." If we are honest, everyone fears this loss, but after a severe trauma these fears magnify and seem much more threatening. What will happen next? Will my family leave me? Will I lose my job? Will my country be attacked? Will I or my buddies be shot and maimed? To regain a sense of control, people often think that if they can make things happen exactly as they want them to, they will regain control over their lives. Of course that isn't true. Often by trying to control others we only push them away and create the very situation we fear.

So what *can* you control? Only you, your thoughts, your actions and reactions—and sometimes those only tentatively. During combat, your automatic survival responses to an attack were triggered and fostered by your training, so you learned to react without engaging in logical thought first. That training may well have saved your life as well as your unit. But this quick emotional (fear or anger) reaction can be dangerous when you come home and the threat is gone.

A client's husband had recently come home from war and, like many other veterans, he always carried a gun. When his neighbor's dog defecated on his lawn, he pulled out his gun and shot his neighbor. The man was in critical condition for weeks and is now a quadriplegic. My client's husband is serving a twenty-five-year prison sentence as a result of this PTSD-induced incident.

So you see, when you come home from war, it is essential to retrain your brain to switch on logical thought before you act. The tendency toward spousal mistreatment and abuse is very high among military personnel. For this reason, military psychologists have expressed a great need for psychotherapists to work with soldiers and their spouses. If you fear hurting someone else, please seek help immediately.

8. Suffers more frequent illnesses. If the trauma occurred some time ago, you may have suffered more illnesses than usual since the event. You, as a combatant, are left with a body on permanent high alert, sometimes for days, months, or years. While at one time it might have saved your life, in the long run, extended stress destabilizes the human immune system.

When you are under stress, the stress hormone cortisol floods your body. A continued and prolonged increase in cortisol eventually breaks down cells and affects every organ, degrading the immune system and making you more vulnerable to disease. The body pumps out too many immune cells called cytokines, which attack you rather than protect you. A correlation between cardiovascular disease and anger has also been found.

9. Shows signs of depression and anxiety.
Depression: If you are not sure whether you are depressed, please read the following questions and answer them truthfully. If your answers are mostly "yes" please seek help with your VA or medical doctor. I will discuss steps you can take to help decrease your depression in Part Two.

- Has anyone told you that you seem depressed, distant, and apathetic much of the time?
- Have you lost interest or pleasure in most activities and people, and would prefer to isolate yourself?
- Have you had a significant weight loss or gain, or decrease or increase in appetite?
- Do you suffer from insomnia or sleep too much most nights?
- Do your muscles twitch or move too slowly? Are you fatigued and low on energy?
- Do you feel worthless or guilty much of the time?
- Are your thoughts mostly negative?

- Do you have difficulty thinking clearly, concentrating, or making decisions?
- Do you often think about dying or suicide?

Anxiety:
Until 2013, PTSD was classified as an anxiety disorder in the *DSM*. Since then it has been reclassified under "Trauma and Stressor Related Disorders."

The following are the most common symptoms of anxiety:

- Motor tension issues: (a) trembling, twitching, or feeling shaky; (b) tense and sore muscles; (c) restlessness and fatigue
- Autonomic nervous system hyperactivity: (a) shortness of breath or smothering sensations; (b) accelerated heart rate; (c) sweating, dizziness; (d) nausea, stomachache, diarrhea, dry mouth; (e) flushes or chills; (f) frequent urination; (g) trouble swallowing or "lump in throat"
- Hyper-vigilance: (a) feeling on edge; (b) exaggerated startle response; (c) difficulty concentrating or "mind going blank"; (d) trouble falling or staying asleep; (e) irritability
- Anxiety sufferers describe their symptoms as comparable to those after drinking too many cups of coffee or caffeine-containing sodas.

10. Abuses drugs and alcohol.
It is common for military personnel and veterans to resort to using legal or illegal drugs and alcohol to help them numb

their feelings and pain. In recent wars many soldiers have been prescribed drugs by physicians to reduce anxiety, depression, and sleeplessness, and to stop physical pain. We are very fortunate to have these drugs, but some veterans have learned to rely solely on them to relieve their symptoms and have become addicted instead of investing in real recovery.

One of my clients credited alcohol with actually saving his life. Of course, knowing what drinking and drugs do to people, I was skeptical. He explained that the only way he had survived during and after the war was to drink and take drugs. He was sure he would have killed himself if he had had no way out of the physical and emotional pain at the time. But his addictions created many more problems than they solved. He lost his friends, his wife, his children, and his job. In the end, to survive, he stopped drinking and taking drugs, sought therapy, and joined both Alcoholics and Narcotics Anonymous.

11. Experiences feelings of guilt and shame or self-blame. These feelings occur when the person feels s/he did something wrong. Serving in Vietnam, Brett lost several friends when the rest of the unit was unable to reach them in time to save them. He blamed himself. Joe, introduced earlier, carried horrendous guilt about burning villages and firing on innocent Vietnamese. Traditionally our society and religions have taught us not to kill, especially innocent children and women. But in recent wars it has been difficult to distinguish real enemies from imagined ones. Even women and children may be armed. This has created a moral dilemma for soldiers not faced in past conflicts. War tends to bring out the dark side in people, and to feel guilty after combat is very common. Some people call this guilt a "soul pain." I will further address this issue in the section on spirituality in Part Two.

12. Has difficulty trusting others, and often questions God. It is normal and human to question. If you believe in God, at first you may have been enormously grateful that God spared your life, but then doubts appear. What kind of a God would have allowed this to happen? You see your fellow troops being wounded or killed and begin to ask, "Will God continue to protect me?"

For many years Mother Teresa lived amid continuous trauma and its effects, working as a missionary and healer in India. I used to wonder how she could continue trusting God after all she saw. I was sure I wouldn't be able to, under similar circumstances. After her death, a section of her journal was released to the public that revealed her doubts and struggles. Was there a loving God? Who was this God, anyway? Knowing Mother Teresa had grappled with the same issues the rest of us humans do made me admire her courage that much more.

If these symptoms begin to interfere with your serenity and your daily functioning, you are likely experiencing PTS. Many people keep their inner turmoil secret and begin to isolate themselves. Don't. Regardless of who you are, male or female, reactions to severe stress are normal and predictable. But the syndrome can quickly worsen into a disorder if you don't do something to alleviate the symptoms now.

What happens in the brain and body during and after a severe trauma?

Here is a simple drawing of the parts of the brain to explain how trauma, stress, and PTSD work. Of course the brain is not nearly as simple as I'm making it, but this diagram will help you understand the causes of some of your symptoms, and that they are normal for the type of trauma you have experienced.

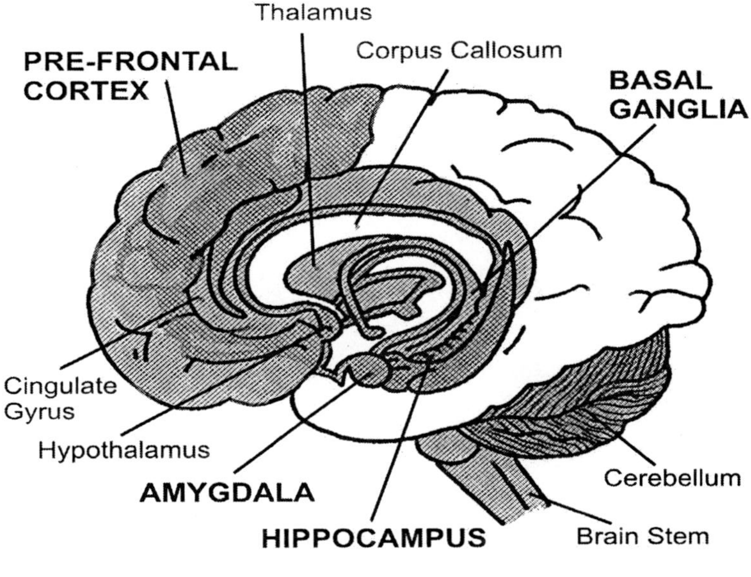
Thalamus
Corpus Callosum
PRE-FRONTAL CORTEX
BASAL GANGLIA
Cingulate Gyrus
Hypothalamus
AMYGDALA
HIPPOCAMPUS
Cerebellum
Brain Stem

Limbic system=amygdala + hippocampus: A group of interconnected structures that mediate emotions, learning, and memory.

Amygdala: Center of emotions. Controls fear response and determines level of threat. It processes reflexive and instinctual emotions (the survival instincts) like fear and anxiety. Learning and memory are activated here as well. In brain imaging research, scientists have found that severe stress lowers the threshold of the amygdala's response to fear stimuli.

Hippocampus: Plays a significant role in the formation of long term memory. Neuroscientists are finding that the hippocampus is smaller in people with PTSD than in other people, due to continued severe stress responses in the brain.

Prefrontal cortex: The thinking part of the brain that controls impulses, attention span, focusing, organizing, and follow-through. Believed to be the area of the brain that developed last in evolution, the prefrontal cortex plans, sets goals, judges priorities, and allows us to suppress troubling memories and thoughts.

Basal ganglia: These control the body's "idling speed." When the basal ganglia are overactive, anxiety, panic, fearfulness, and conflict avoidance are often the result.

Remember, the brain is a physical organ just like your heart, your lungs, or your kidneys. Its purpose is to regulate the emotions, thoughts, memories, and nervous system. As soon as a real or imagined threat is perceived either consciously or unconsciously, as in PTS, your brain chemistry changes and the levels of adrenaline, norepinephrine, and cortisol increase. The brain's chief emotional center, the amygdala, which carries the survival instincts and reflexive emotions such as fear and anxiety, is activated. It tells you how to react to a situation before you have conscious thought. The amygdala also keeps track of all your past good and bad feelings about memories, but not the facts such as names, time frame, and location.

That is the job of the hippocampus. The hippocampus keeps track of the facts, but not the feelings, and plays a significant role in the formation of long term memory. Then, if need be, it sends these facts on to the prefrontal cortex, or thinking part of the brain, to plan, set goals, and judge priorities. If the hippocampus is overwhelmed by stress hormones, it loses the ability to separate time, and during a flashback you actually believe "then" is "now."

When the automatic, inborn survival instinct called the "freeze, fight or flight response" is activated by a real or perceived threat, the body directs most of the oxygen and blood to the brain stem and amygdala (emotional brain), not to the hippocampus and the prefrontal cortex that modulate the amygdala. The alarm sounds for only a thousandth of a second before the amygdala takes command and shuts down the hippocampus and the prefrontal cortex. The shut-down happens so quickly that there is no time to assess the threat logically. The body freezes for a moment, then fights or runs. Watch a frightened deer. It freezes, then darts away. This temporary immobility allows the body to marshal enormous amounts of energy before it acts.

The amygdala sends panic messages into the rest of the brain, especially to the hippocampus. It becomes hyperactive and sears fragments of memory onto the mind with a force that's hard to extinguish. When a trigger in the present, such as a noise or smell, is associated with a past trauma, the past event reignites in the present, taking the shape of nightmares and flashbacks. Remember the early behavioral studies Pavlov performed on dogs? The researchers rang a bell, then gave the dog a treat. Soon all the researchers had to do was ring the bell and the dog began to salivate, even without the treat. That's how a gunshot may cause a PTS reaction such as a flashback, a memory, and a physical reaction. Your mind has paired the gunshot with danger from the past. Because of this intricate set of connections in the brain, the activation of one memory automatically triggers comparable memories and evokes similar feelings, both emotional and physical.

The amygdala has no way of tracking names, time, or place. However it remembers bad feelings as though they are now. So in flashbacks, when something triggers a bad memory, the person goes right back to the past as though it is the present.

Why has the brain evolved in this way? Think of the so-called good old days when all those lions and tigers and bears out there in a hostile environment were waiting to eat us for dinner. Over time, the human body developed a system to protect us from these threats. As the body evolved to help itself survive, it developed a nervous system to alert people to danger. Adrenaline and cortisol, called stress hormones, are pumped into the organs, including the brain stem and the emotional centers in the brain, to increase the heart rate, make the breath come faster, tense the muscles, and make us alert and miraculously strong, ready to fight or run.

Normally, if the person escaped from the predator and the real or perceived threat ended, the adrenaline and cortisol levels receded to a balanced amount in the body. The sudden surges in chemicals, and then the return to a balanced state, both saved the person's life and actually helped the body tune itself up, just like when we take a car on a highway and run it at high speed.

Animals have a similar freeze, fight or flight system in their bodies and react to threats in similar ways to humans. If you watch *Animal Planet* on television, or Cesar Millan, or have read Temple Grandin's books, such as *Animals Make Us Human*, you will discover stories of severely abused dogs, or dogs in wartime, that contracted PTS and even PTSD. One such story involves a German Shepherd that helped soldiers find IEDs in Iraq. The dog was a great warrior, carefully selected and trained, and very successful in saving people's lives. But after encountering continued explosions for years, it lapsed into PTSD and was sent home. A year later it still shook, cowered, and hid, terrified of touch when triggered by certain noises. Does this sound familiar?

Contrary to how we often see ourselves, the physical body, emotions, and mind are not independent entities. All are irrevocably connected to the brain, a physical organ that maintains continuous close communication and feedback loops among the various elements. Without the brain, the body, emotions, and thoughts as we know them would not exist. Our thoughts and emotions are actually seated in distinct areas within the brain and are greatly influenced by physical components such as hormones, enzymes, and proteins that are generated within the body.

In his book *Change Your Brain, Change Your Life,* Daniel G. Amen, M.D., describes how he used a brain SPECT (3-D imaging technique) to find that, compared to other people, a veteran with severe PTSD had markedly increased left-side activity in the basal ganglia (a collection of nuclei outside and above the limbic system). This type of basal ganglia activity is generally associated with chronic irritability or anger. Dr. Amen speculated that the veteran's thirteen-month war experience had set the basal ganglia to be on constant alert. The veteran had never learned how to reset his brain back to normal.

Usually when the threat is gone, the adrenaline and cortisol surges end and the brain resets itself. But when a person has had to live under constant threat and crisis, as many veterans have for months or years, the body becomes addicted to the surges of adrenaline as it would to a drug, and craves to get back to that level of excitement (fear and excitement create very similar effects in the body). Life becomes meaningless without that constant adrenaline rush. Many veterans feel useless when they come home, and sign up for another tour of duty or become policemen or emergency technicians in an effort to regain a sense of purpose. For example, one of the veterans I counseled became an FBI agent and worked undercover.

During the time of crisis, people become detached and live in denial of what might happen to them. With many of the people I treated for PTSD, I found that when their bodies believed they were no longer in danger, they began to release the emotions they had hidden in order to function during the war. Many soldiers built firewalls around themselves while in combat. At the time, the walls served them well. However, when they came home, for many the walls collapsed. This is not an unusual occurrence for returned veterans.

A young veteran who had served as a nurse in Iraq told me, "Sure, I saw a lot of gruesome things, but I had no problems during the year I was in Iraq. I just did my job and went on my way. It wasn't until after I came back that I started having nightmares. The nightmares were always of soldiers screaming and bleeding to death. In my dreams, I would try so hard to get to my patients, but couldn't get to them in time to save them. My husband would wake me and hold me for a while until I stopped shaking. It seemed to me that my mind felt safe enough to release the fears and memories I had held in my body, and only then I was able to deal with the trauma of working with continual life-and-death situations."

Which military personnel are most affected by PTS or PTSD in War?

Anyone who is caught in the trauma of war is affected. Combatants, first responders, medical staff, and military personnel other than combatants are all affected by war. Personnel of both sexes and all ages, races, intellects, and education levels are affected. Studies indicate that women are twice as susceptible to PTSD than men. That may well indicate a brain difference. However, men have more of a tendency to hide and repress their feelings than women do, and many men won't report their symptoms in order to receive help. They tend to use alcohol and drugs more frequently and /or release their feelings in bouts of anger.

Most humans respond in a similar way to trauma, even those who have been labeled as our enemies. I recently heard a report on CNN that said many Taliban leaders and Islamic combatants are now suffering severely from PTSD. Whether that is comforting or alarming to you, it nevertheless demonstrates the universality of this phenomenon.

I would be remiss if I didn't add another category to the list of military personnel affected by PTS and PTSD. Sadly, the statistics from the Department of Defense indicate that

23,000 sexual assaults occurred in the military in 2011 alone, and that only about 13% were reported. As documented in the film *Raped in the Ranks*, one of every three women in the military is sexually assaulted. Another study indicates that 23% of women in the military report sexual assault. However, contrary to what many people believe, this is not a problem that affects only women. Recent studies have determined that over half of the people in the military who are raped are men.

The military is not prepared, and frequently not willing, to deal with the problem. According to several veterans, the personnel in charge often act annoyed when these incidents are reported, and the victims are left in shock, unprotected, without justice, and without counseling. Often they are dismissed from the military or do not receive promotions. Because of the treatment they know they will receive both by their superiors and the others in their unit, many do not report sexual assault or harassment. The men and women in this situation have few alternatives.

One of the female veterans I spoke to told me her story. One evening she had hurried to the bathroom to clean up before bed. Suddenly she had been tackled from behind by two soldiers stinking of liquor. She screamed, but no one came to her aid. One officer rushed by but did nothing. The two men beat her and brutally raped her, then left her by the side of the path. When she reported the rape, the officer who interviewed her warned her not to pursue it. He said it would only cause trouble for her and the rest of the unit.

The depth of trauma that occurs from rape is immense. Very few soldiers would stand by and allow a person in their unit to shoot one of their own. Yet what happens during rape is similar. Many people say they would rather have been killed than raped.

So how can we stop this crime from occurring? At present around fifty thousand men are being treated by the VA for sexual assault. The military is educating all troops about sexual assault. The U. S. Senate is changing the laws concerning rape, and President Obama has spoken out for harsh punishment of offenders.

All veterans need to know about a recent program established by Leon Panetta to provide advocates for rape survivors, called the Victims Assistance Organization. However, the crime must be reported before treatment can be accessed.

Active-duty soldiers and veterans alike are a large part of the answer. **Much of the problem deals with people's attitude toward rape.** Many do not see it as a "real" crime that creates horrendous pain and lifelong severe trauma for the victim. Rape is dismissed with a shrug or a laugh. "Boys will be boys," they say. Others, because of the probable negative consequences, are afraid to stand up to offenders and therefore say nothing.

Veterans like you, both men and women, who are able to empathize with the rape victim, abhor what is going on in the military. You understand that it might have been you, or someone you love, who was victimized. Over the years I have heard of units where one or two men speak privately to the others and secretly unite to develop a plan and a signal so they can protect each other. Your power is in numbers and your close relationships with one another. You know how to work as a team and fight together. These are some of your greatest strengths. Use these strengths to help each other.

Treatment for the survivors, education, and deterrents for crimes such as rape are essential, but it is also time to work to change our culture. Help transform the attitudes of all personnel, combat troops, and the public on the severe trauma and consequences of rape, and demand changes in the military. Work with your legislators to take the reporting and the judicial process out of the hands of the chain of command.

Veterans, take the crime of rape seriously and stand up together. For you who have been sexually assaulted, follow the steps in Part Two of this book to help you deal with the trauma. Women especially should read *Women Under Fire: Abuse in the Military* by Sarah Blum, a former nurse in Vietnam. *Women Under Fire* details Blum's true story and the stories of other women who were raped or otherwise sexually assaulted in the military. She is working on a second book, *Women Under Fire: PTSD and Healing*. Remember, you are not alone and you don't need to suffer alone. Empower yourself and do something to assist yourself and other survivors.

PART TWO

Twenty Steps to Help You Heal

These steps to recovery have been placed in the approximate order you will need to practice them in order to heal. But you don't have to do all of them, or learn them in the order presented, if that doesn't serve you. For now, only practice those steps that you are drawn to and feel you need. Later you may wish to try some others as well.

The Healing Wall, Part II
by Patrick Overton, Vietnam veteran

II.
I visited the Wall.
One evening in the late summer of the year,
when the cool winds blew across the Mall and the
early evening sun was crisp, I went to the Wall, again.
I stood where I had stood before but refused to go,
and without ever deciding,
without ever giving consent
I found myself moving toward it,
pulled by some force I could not see,
drawn by memories I could no longer deny.
I began the slow descent into the dark hole,
not wanting to but needing to go back into
what I had spent twenty-five years trying to forget.

It's time to deal with your trauma.

As you can see from the poem "The Healing Wall," written by Vietnam veteran Patrick Overton, many veterans have a hard time honestly facing how their war experiences are influencing their current lives. It is easier to pretend that the symptoms they've had since the trauma of war don't hold any power over their everyday lives.

If you are like most veterans, it is usually your family and friends who see most clearly the pain and problems you are facing. Because they love you and want you to recover, they may also be the ones who confront you most often about the issues they have observed since your return. Don't ignore them. Listen to your loved ones and carefully evaluate what they say to see whether they are right.

If one of the troops in your unit had warned you that the enemy was waiting for you in a house down the street, would you have denied it? If so, what do you think might have happened? I understand that facing your issues takes a lot of courage, but you probably realize by now that running away from problems or pretending they don't exist won't work to improve your relationships, your job, or your emotional and physical health.

Profile of a Resilient Person

Resilient people are like young, flexible trees.
They can twist in a storm, but do not snap.
Instead they spring back when the storm is over.

Your goal in recovery will be to alleviate, or at least diminish, the symptoms of PTS that you have identified in the symptom list in Part One of this book. Now that you have identified the feelings and behaviors that you no longer want in your life, it is time to look at what you need to learn to help you become more resilient to stress in the future.

Here are some characteristics that researchers have discovered occur most frequently in resilient people who can comfortably deal with stress. To some degree these are genetic, but research also shows that you can cultivate these characteristics to master any crisis. Whether they are based in genetics or are learned over time doesn't matter. You can practice and learn them now. Don't give up. You didn't learn to read and write in a day. Remember how many years it took you to develop your present patterns of behavior.

CHARACTERISTICS OF RESILIENT PEOPLE

- They stay connected to others.
- They are optimistic.
- They are spiritual.
- They are playful and enjoy themselves as children do. They wonder about things, experiment, and laugh.
- They pick their battles. They focus on things over which they have some influence and not on things they can't control.
- They give back to others.
- They stay as healthy as possible.
- They find the silver linings in problems.
- They gain strength from adversity.

WHAT MAKES PEOPLE HAPPY?

Contrary to what many people in Western culture believe, researchers have found that what the majority of people around the world say makes them most happy is not having more things, but rather the quality of their social relationships.

The following are some of the common answers:

- Connection with people you love
- Innovative change, or excitement
- A challenge that makes you stretch to the point where you experience the best of yourself
- Creative expression, such as art, music, gardening, or imagining new ways of doing something

- Meaning and contribution: Do I matter? Have I contributed to this world? As a veteran, you may have felt you mattered during the war. But now?

Following are twenty steps that will help you even if you evaluate that your trauma is not very severe. They could change your life. Give them a try.

STEP ONE:

Become stable.

Before you move on to any other steps, please ask yourself whether you are stable and functional enough to be safe. If the answer is no, make an appointment with your VA before you do anything else. If you are in a rural area, contact the Veteran's Center, a community-based treatment program financed by the VA but independently operated. One of the Afghanistan veterans I interviewed said that his experience with the Veteran's Center had been terrific. Most of the counselors he saw were Vietnam veterans who traveled weekly to his rural area in a motor home. They helped him deal with his PTSD symptoms and readjust to civilian life.

Flashbacks, nightmares, and vivid memories devastate veterans emotionally. The intense fear that rips through their bodies when they are triggered (activated) to relive their war traumas are the hardest to handle when they come home, but they are also the greatest motivators for change. You've heard the phrase, "No pain, no gain." I don't believe that the saying is true in all cases, but often it is.

As discussed in Part One, when the repercussions of the trauma are triggered afterward, the amygdala (emotional center of the brain) sends panicked messages to other areas in the brain, including the hippocampus, the brain's center for storing long-term memories. Past events reignite in the present and create intense memories, nightmares, and flashbacks. For some veterans these repercussions come several times a day; for others, weekly; for still others, rarely; but when they come, they may be strong enough to immobilize a person.

Until you are able to calm yourself and disengage yourself enough from these emotional memories to make life manageable, it will be hard to practice any of the steps in this book. Although flashbacks rarely occur for people who have PTS (as opposed to PTSD), bad memories and nightmares are common. Please spend as much time practicing the suggestions in Step One as you need to feel some sense of control over your symptoms before moving on to the other steps.

As a PTS or PTSD sufferer, the biggest hurdle you face is to be able to separate the past from the present, so that you can see that your flashbacks or nightmares are merely memories and that you are safe now. Remember that the amygdala (emotional center) and the hippocampus are being triggered. To bring you back to reality and into the present, you must learn to reactivate your prefrontal-cortex (thinking, reasoning center) in order to get in touch with the facts, time frame, and location of your current reality.

1. **Program your mind.** Your mind is literal and will gradually learn to believe whatever you tell it. Before you experience a flashback or dream, remind yourself frequently throughout the day, "I am not in Afghanistan now. I am home. I am

safe," or any other reassuring words that help you feel safe. Repeat this frequently, so that your unconscious mind will begin to believe what you are saying. Say it out loud so you can literally hear your own words. Try this technique a hundred times a day. Place the words on file cards and tape them to your mirrors, dashboard, TV, etc. That way you can read them wherever you go.

2. Stop and think before you act. In an instant, your brain sizes up a situation. If it decides the situation resembles the trauma you experienced previously (by sight, sound, smell, taste, or feel) and that you are in danger, you experience intense fear. Your body reacts immediately by getting ready to fight or run. Your muscles tense, your heart races, and time seems to stand still. This process is like a feedback loop that happens so rapidly, most people are unaware of it.

First and foremost, you need to know that, as a child, you gradually learned that, rather than react immediately to a trigger, you needed to take a moment to allow the prefrontal cortex (logical brain) to assess your situation and then act. You learned to ask questions of yourself, such as, "Is this threat real?" If the answer was yes, you then asked, "What is my best course of action?" By the time you were an adult, you were able to control most of your impulses.

When people have not learned impulse control (and/or occasionally when terrified), they do what the old adage says: "Shoot first and ask questions later."

In your military training, you were taught to override the prefrontal cortex and respond without logical thought. In many combat situations you were in mortal danger and would not have survived if you hadn't reverted to the automatic survival responses of the body under threat. But now that you are home again, you will need to unlearn what you learned in wartime and retrain your brain to take a few seconds to assess the situation, come up with a solution, and then act (not react). It's not easy, but you learned it as a child, and you can do it again.

Recall the earlier example of the veteran who shot his neighbor when the man's dog defecated on the veteran's lawn. If the veteran had learned to stop acting on impulse and think first, he would not be serving a life sentence in prison.

Here are some ways to help you retrain yourself to think logically before acting:

- Talk to yourself silently, or even out loud if you need to. Let your mind know, several times a day, that you are safe now, that you have the time to think before you act. You are home, not in a war zone.
- Usually military personnel, when they first come home or even much later, startle easily and react immediately. Observe yourself throughout the day. Whenever you jump, tell yourself, "STOP. THINK." Don't act immediately. Ask yourself, "What startled me?" Was it truly dangerous? What should you do about it? If it is nothing dangerous, tell yourself, "I'm safe. I'm all right. I'm home now. Relax." Then breathe in and out deeply and slowly, allowing yourself to relax. Continue with this practice whenever you feel startled, for as long as it takes to become less reactive.

- If you need to, substitute a sound for an automatic action. Making a sound will give your prefrontal cortex more time to think logically. For example, one of the Marines I counseled tried to change his actions with thoughts alone, but was unable to stop when he felt threatened. Usually he raised his fists and punched before he could think. He realized that thinking alone wouldn't do the trick. He needed to substitute a different action for punching. So he learned to shout instead of punch (presumed threat—shout, instead of presumed threat—punch). In the split second it took to shout, his logical brain kicked into gear and he was able to stop the punch.

3. When you have a bad memory or feel yourself heading into a flashback, always first make sure that you are safe. Check around you. When you have determined you are safe, think of the trauma as if it were happening long ago, not right now. Teach your mind to separate the past from the present.

4. After the flashback, use your logical brain to determine your body's typical first response signaling you're about to experience a flashback or vivid memory. Does your heart race? Do you sweat or shake? What do you feel as you head into a flashback? Make the thoughts clear in your mind. "I am shaking and sweating because I'm remembering that I was afraid during the attack in Fallujah three years ago. This is a memory." Understanding how your emotions and your body interact will sensitize you to your body's signals, eventually leading you to a point where you can control an oncoming flashback, or avoid it completely.

If you don't yet recognize these physical signals, ask yourself after the flashback, "What happened first?" Usually your mind will tell you. If not, try to picture yourself standing outside of your body on a hill, watching your body below. What is your body experiencing? Gradually you will be able to separate yourself from the trauma long enough to recognize what your body does when your emotions sense a threat.

5. When you prepare for bed, repeat the words, "I am home; I am safe" several times before you go to sleep. Your mind is more powerful than you can imagine. Ask your mind honestly to help you, and it will. But don't expect immediate results. Retraining your mind takes time.

Tell your mind, "I am able to intrude on my dream with my waking mind and consciously change my dreams." In time the logical mind will be able to watch your dream and make your emotional mind aware that you are safe and that the dream isn't real. You want the dream to end. At that point, you will usually wake up.

6. Write down your memory, dream, or flashback after it occurs and refer to it clearly as happening in the past. "It is just a memory." Distance yourself from it. Don't allow it to stay in your mind as though it's a reality now. "That was a year ago, March 25th at six p.m., in Afghanistan. I am not there now. Today is April 4th at 2 p.m. in Idaho. I am home now. I am safe." Shift your attention outside of yourself. Look at your clothes. You are not in uniform now. Look around the room and identify specific objects that are different than the things you saw in Afghanistan. By thinking these thoughts, you are helping the hippocampus to engage.

Remind yourself that you survived. In her book *8 Keys to Safe Trauma Recovery*, well-known psychotherapist and trauma recovery specialist Babette Rothschild, LCSW, advises, "Write your epilogue first." What she means is that usually when people journal or talk about their trauma, they begin the story just before the actual event and then recount the details as they remember them happening. Often, however, they get stuck somewhere in the middle of the trauma and never get to the end and beyond, all the way to the present. So the mind forgets they survived and keeps them "trapped" in the trauma. Rothschild advises that you begin the story in the present. Start with now or a significant point after the trauma, and work back to the trauma. This approach will remind you that indeed you did survive.

7. If you are driving a car or working on dangerous machinery when you get a signal that you are about to go into a flashback or vivid memory, stop what you are doing and move to a place of safety. If you are somewhere where you can safely lie down on a sofa, a bed, the floor, or the ground, do so.

8. Immediately reassure yourself that you are not in the traumatic situation now and you are safe. Repeat several times, "I am home (or wherever). I am safe now. I survived." If you believe in a higher power, ask that power for help. Use your senses of sight, hearing, smell, sound, and touch to convince your mind you are not experiencing the trauma now. "I see the swing my kids play on every day. I see my neighbor's green car. I hear the sound of children playing. I smell soup cooking. I am touching grass. I am touching my jeans." Remind yourself that the flashback comes from the emotional brain, the amygdala, but you have a logical higher brain that can help you see that you are no longer there. Trust it.

9. After the dream or flashback, lean back and give your body permission to feel what it needs to feel. For example, let yourself shake. The body has natural means of dealing with stress, and shaking is one of them. Tears are another. Have you ever watched your dog shake after a trauma? Or a child burst into tears after being frightened? We'll discuss these natural reactions in more depth later. For now, know that when you stop fighting against the natural reactions of your body and emotions, you lessen the stress.

10. For many people, breathing through the re-experienced trauma is very helpful. Breathe slowly, steadily, and evenly, all the way in and all the way out, centering your thoughts on your chest and hearing the sound of your breath coming in and out. This deep-breathing exercise will help you relax enough to get to the other side without severe effects.

11. Find an object that helps you relax. Find a sea shell, a special rock, a polished stone, a ball, or anything else that you value and that centers you. Keep it in your pocket and touch it often throughout the day when you feel relaxed, so you connect the object with a sense of being okay. As soon as you feel yourself slipping into a memory or flashback, touch the object and feel yourself relax. The object serves as an anchor to the real world, here and now.

12. Record calming music or a reassuring message on your cell phone or digital recorder. The message can be in your own voice or that of someone you love. Choose a sound that helps you stay in the present. Play it when you notice the first signs of a flashback and let the soothing words and voice bring your mind back to the present. You can also create a calming tape or use calming music at night, before you go to sleep.

13. Use a nightlight if it helps to bring you back to reality after you wake up from a nightmare. Complete darkness can often trigger fear when you wake up and don't recognize where you are. Your mind believes there is an enemy threatening you. A nightlight can help you see your surroundings and remember you are safe at home.

14. If these guidelines don't work, ask for help from someone you trust who is likely to be present when nightmares or flashbacks occur, like your spouse or partner. Discuss with him or her how he or she can help you. For example, your partner could gently repeat, over and over if necessary, "You are home now. You are not in Iraq. You are safe." If you can tolerate being touched, let the person hold you or touch your arm, centering you in the present. Ask her or him to repeat, "I am here. Hear my voice. Feel my hand. Look around you. See the bed, the table, the sofa. See the tree outside our window."

15. Always talk to your children about what is happening to you. Tell them how they can help you. If you do not become violent when you enter a flashback or nightmare, you might tell them they can help you by touching you gently and saying, "Daddy, Daddy. We're home. I'm here." If you are afraid of becoming violent, you may want to tell them they need to leave the room, that you will be okay, and you will come to get them when the memory is over. Always reassure them that this is about the war and has nothing to do with them. It is not their fault.

16. Instead of avoiding intimidating places altogether, slowly explore them in safety with someone you trust, like a mate or a friend. If you live or work in an environment that triggers you frequently, find ways to modify it without isolating yourself or leaving. You might use sound-dampening earphones, ear plugs, etc., to block out triggering noises. But if you can't stay, don't punish yourself. Leave, as Joe did when he left the sawmill located next to the gun range. Plan to re-expose yourself gradually and in a safe manner when you are ready to do so. (Check Step Eleven to learn more about Prolonged Exposure Therapy.)

17. Be discerning about using the Internet as well as watching movies and TV programs. Sensory overload will increase your anxiety and trigger flashbacks. Set boundaries around technology. Turn off your computer and TV, and learn to quiet your mind instead. Seeing violent images and hearing screaming may trigger you unnecessarily. For example, many veterans experienced flashbacks while watching the movie

Saving Private Ryan. I would suggest you only see a movie like that with a counselor present to provide immediate help, should you need it.

18. To get past the "freeze" response of your body, literally get moving. When you feel immobilized, move your legs and arms, walk, run, do gentle exercises. Your mind will follow your body.

19. If you are really serious about recovery, don't carry firearms. If you do, keep the bullets or firing pin in a different pocket than your gun. Although it is legal for you to carry a loaded weapon when you come home, until you are at a point where you can take time to assess a problem before you act, having immediate access to a loaded gun can put you and others at great risk. Depending on where you live, you will very rarely need a gun to protect yourself, now that you are home.

My client's husband, a Vietnam war veteran, shot and killed a man in a bar when the man made fun of his uniform. Then there was the veteran who shot his neighbor when his neighbor's dog defecated on his lawn. Neither would be spending the rest of their lives in prison if they had not had immediate access to a loaded gun. And last of all, remember the young man who played Russian roulette with his Iraq veteran buddies. He would probably still be alive if he had not carried a loaded gun.

Statistics indicate that most people killed by gunshot wounds are loved ones mistaken for a perpetrator or enemy. If you feel you absolutely need to carry a gun, don't load it and/or remove the firing pin and put it in your pocket. Yes, it will take a little time to reload the weapon or to replace the firing pin, but by that time your logical mind will most likely be in control again and you can make an informed decision. Still, it's a big risk. If you can manage to get along without a firearm, do so. Instead, carry a tazer or pepper spray if you feel too vulnerable without any protection. They are not lethal.

20. If you are stressed, take time to get away into nature and decompress. For some ideas on how to do this, look at Step Fifteen.

Some counselors believe that you should deal with your memories and emotions immediately following a trauma. But until you feel stable enough to cope with them, this may not be the right time for you, and the memories may cause you to become even more dysfunctional. With time, you will be able to separate the past from the present and distance yourself from the memories enough so the mind and body won't react as if the trauma is occurring now. At that time, you can deal with the memories. In the meantime, if you feel compelled to talk about your trauma, check Step Nine for some techniques to cope with memories and emotions.

STEP TWO:
Remain connected to others.

Few other steps are as important as this one. Frequently when troops come home, following a short honeymoon period where they, their families, and their friends are excited to reconnect with one another, veterans begin to feel alienated, misunderstood, and lonely, as if they don't belong. To some degree, they are right. Though all PTS sufferers exhibit similar symptoms, the circumstances of war are unique. Combat is a unique situation, and no one will understand you and what you went through like another veteran.

Especially now, when the U. S. military consists of professional warriors instead of a general draft, the role of civilian Americans has been reduced to that of well-wishing spectators who are not involved in the war. Except for families and friends of volunteer servicemen and -women, citizens at large know little and understand even less about what is happening to the troops overseas.

During the Vietnam war, many Americans at home felt intimately involved in the war. Not only did they have loved ones overseas, but the nightly news regularly displayed photos and films taken at the battlefield. We all shared in that war because the images were always in our minds. Rightly or wrongly, the politics of the war angered some people, but when we saw photos of the coffins coming home, we felt shocked and grieved. Now civilians are no longer included in the lives of our soldiers.

When interviewed in 2010 by Chief Military Correspondent David Wood, almost without exception, the troops said they were excited about what they were doing and felt a pride in their mission even after two or three deployments. However, as many veterans came home to stay, they felt as if they had no purpose in life. After years of discipline and service, sharing the intensity of combat and the experience of depending on each other to stay alive, soldiers came home to what many considered a money-driven, self-centered society with a lack of discipline and lax values. Some decided to re-enlist to regain purpose and to avoid dealing with the seemingly insurmountable problems of returning home.

When I talked to one of the veterans about his experience of coming home to his wife, he said, "We have nothing in common anymore. What can I say to her? She doesn't want to hear about the war, and that's all I know. And all she wants to talk about is the kids and buying a different house. I can't help it. I look at her life as trivial."

So how did he react to this situation?

Like many others who terminate active duty, he began to isolate himself. By the word "isolate" I do not mean moving into the mountains, far away from others. I am speaking more of mental and emotional withdrawal and isolation.

It is valuable to take time in nature from time to time, away from the hustle and bustle of the city, to decompress and listen to the birds and the trees in the wind, to go fishing and hiking. If you were not given the opportunity to let your guard down and reintegrate slowly after you returned from a war zone, do so now. However, after a few days or weeks in nature, it will be time to return to civilization.

Even though you might feel like it, **don't isolate yourself.** Humans are social beings and need companionship and support. It's the way we evolved. We now know how very important it is for anyone—but especially you, as a veteran—to connect to others when you come home. Don't allow your trauma to disrupt your social relationships.

According to recent research cited in Gabor Maté's book *When the Body Says No*, people who have a good support system of friends and family with whom they can share feelings and activities are happier and become ill less frequently. Those without such a support system when under chronic stress exhibit suppressed immune systems and are often tired and ill.

You need at least one close relationship with someone who cares about you, just the way you are, and with whom you can truly be yourself and share your innermost feelings and thoughts without being judged. People who maintain an impersonal distance from everyone may have many so-called "friends," but say they are lonely. Often the person you reach out to will be another veteran, because he or she understands what you have experienced and will actually "hear" you.

Reaching out to others takes a lot of courage, but as a veteran you are familiar with what it takes to be courageous. Think back to a time during the war when you were courageous. What happened? Usually it meant doing something you would rather not do, but you did it anyway. When my clients told me how hard it was to stay in touch with others, I would empathize with them, and then I would say, "If you really want to get better, do it anyway."

You are not a victim at present. You are an adult and you can choose in what direction you will go, up or down. Here are some ways that will help you return and reconnect to the civilian world.

1. Find a companion you can trust and talk to about what is going on inside. Some people feel compelled to tell their story to an empathic ear immediately after the trauma. If this is you, look for someone you can trust who will not judge you, but will listen instead of giving advice. Research has shown that keeping secrets is unhealthy.

The act of keeping a secret about a traumatizing event can cause even more damage than experiencing the event itself. Have you ever heard the saying, "Confession is good for the soul?" Psychologist James Pennebaker, in a lengthy study, determined that when clients told their secrets, their health improved and measurable decreases in their stress hormone levels occurred.

If you don't have anyone to turn to, and you feel too vulnerable to talk openly with people, find an animal to talk to. Many of my clients have developed close friendships with horses, dogs, cats, or even rabbits. They talk to them, tell them their worst experiences, confide their dreams, and stroke and touch them. Regardless of what you say to an animal, it will love you and accept you. Regardless of what secrets you tell it, you will bond with each other. Bonding with an animal is a very important step that has even helped people decide not to end their lives. If you live somewhere you can't own a pet, consider volunteering at a nearby animal shelter.

Recently I met a woman during a book signing for one of my novels. She asked me what I was currently writing. I mentioned this book and she smiled. "Wow," she said. "That's amazing. I work for an organization called Puppies Behind Bars. We teach prisoners to train dogs for disabled veterans, especially for veterans with PTSD." There are also several other organizations that train service dogs for disabled veterans. For a bestselling, heartwarming book of stories about soldiers and their service dogs, read *Soldier Dogs* by Maria Goodavage.

Dogs especially make great companions and can help you through difficult times. One day I took my little dachshund, William Wallace (named after the hero of *Braveheart*), out for a walk in our neighborhood. A large truck passed by. In it sat a tall, handsome young man in uniform, and on his shoulder, nuzzled next to his ear, lay a little sleeping poodle. When I returned home I mentioned the experience to my husband, who had served as a military officer when he was young. The first thing he said was, "Now that's a real man!"

2. Develop relationships with other veterans who understand how you feel and with whom you can share your experiences and feelings. If you don't know any other veterans in your area, call your local VA for connections. A note of caution: if you join a group that does not have a positive attitude or a positive leader, you may actually get more depressed and feel more and more hopeless. Leave the group if you feel that happening and find or form another group.

3. Use Skype to keep in touch with the close friends (brothers and sisters) you developed in the military. Staying in contact via Skype, an inexpensive video-telephone service, will help you through the difficult times. Many veterans say that what they miss most are the friendships they had formed in their units. They miss the closeness and cooperation of sharing mutual experiences in combat. Don't let those friendships go. They will always be important to you. One of my Vietnam-veteran friends and his unit still hold an annual get-together to reminisce, laugh, and cry.

4. Your local VA will usually host a support group that meets regularly. Join it. Usually the group is moderated by a counselor and/or has steps to follow that keep you on track. You will be able to share your experiences and give and receive empathy and understanding, as well as great advice.

5. If you live in a rural location and have no support groups near you, find one on the Internet. There are several. If you have no computer, don't use that as an excuse. You may have access at your public library. Search for "veteran's support groups" in Google or another search engine. Evaluate several sites and their blogs before you decide on the one best for you. Look for bloggers who have similar values to yours, who are empathetic and good at listening, and whose writing makes you feel uplifted and encouraged.

6. Find a local group or organization you can join that has values and interests similar to yours. This can be a church, singles club, political party, chess club, Lions, Elks or Kiwanis Club, honors society, book club, photography club, writers' league, twelve-step program, or any other group you find to be positive and that helps you become the person you want to be.

7. Many people in the military have resorted to drugs and alcohol to deal with their stress. If you have a drug or alcohol problem or are addicted, go to a local VA or community recovery group, or to Alcoholics Anonymous (AA) or Narcotics Anonymous (NA). If your significant other has a drug or alcohol problem, attend a program for family and friends, like Alanon. You will find incredible support and wisdom in most of these groups. If you need to attend for a while before you begin to talk, that's okay. A sponsor can help you. Make sure to study and work on the twelve steps if you decide on AA. These steps have helped millions of people overcome their addictions.

8. Get reacquainted with your significant other and children again. Your spouse and children don't know you anymore, and you don't know them. This is natural, especially after several tours of duty or a couple of years of absence. Even though your children may have talked to you on Skype and may recognize you, that's not the same as living together. Now it is time to get reacquainted with each other.

Take a night out with your mate at least once a week, just the two of you. Do something you both enjoy, like seeing a movie or going out for dinner. Make sure you take time to talk and hold hands. Be respectful and honest with each other. Go back and reminisce about the good times you had before the war. Remember why you fell in love and what you liked about each other. Both of you need to share what happened during the absence, if possible. Share your feelings and dreams for the future. Talk about what has changed. Talk about what you still have in common.

Sometimes it takes a third person to help moderate in a dispute. Find a minister or a counselor to help you. If possible, decide on a divorce or separation only after the two of you have undergone partner counseling.

9. Depending on your children's ages, you may need to start from the beginning. They may barely remember you, and they have adjusted to life with your spouse and without you. Follow her or his rules until you can work out new rules together. Don't expect the children to accept you or listen to you at first. You are a stranger to them. Maybe the only place they have seen you is in photographs and on Skype, and maybe not even there. You need to get to know each other before you can fully become a dad or mom again.

Ask your children what they like to do, what they think of daycare or school, what sports, TV shows, games, books, and toys they like. Take each child out separately and regularly, one-on-one, to do something they love to do. Interact with them even if you don't feel like it. Give yourself permission to become playful again and have fun. If the children are learning to use the computer or ride a bike, join them and teach them, or learn along with them. Teach your children sports and games. Please keep the criticism and rules to a minimum. You are not in the military now. Plan family outings regularly, and attend their recitals and sports events.

A mistake many people make after a severe trauma like war is to not let their children know what is going on. As a result, the experience traumatizes them as well. If you remember my personal story in the introduction, you will understand how your child may be feeling as well. Let your children know that when you have nightmares, get angry, or draw away from them, it's not their fault. Tell them in very general terms what war is about and what is going on with you, so they don't feel they are to blame for your trauma. Say something like, "Jimmy, this has nothing to do with you." Then give a short but honest explanation of what is happening. Let your partner help you when possible.

10. As you become reacquainted with your children, set rational rules and consequences together with your spouse, and support each other in your decisions. If you need to change the rules that have been set in your absence, try not to criticize each other in front of the children. They must know you are a team and that their parents are in charge. Children need limits and consistency, as well as love. It makes them feel secure.

11. Ask for help whenever you need it. Many people are ashamed or afraid to ask for help in case they will be rejected or thought of as weak. However, we live in community and need to depend on each other. If you ask someone for help and she or he says no, ask someone else.

Carefully select the people you will trust. Observe people first before committing to relationships with them. Look for these characteristics of a potential good friend: non-judgmental, empathic, a good listener, keeps confidentiality, does not take advantage of others, open-minded, and centered. Most of all, watch that their actions match their words. Trust someone who says he or she will do something and then does it. Remember the politicians. Do you trust those who say one thing and then, a year or even a day later, say or do the exact opposite?

Love is freely given. Trust is earned.

STEP THREE:

Empower yourself.

Often after veterans come home and try to reintegrate into society, they feel helpless to change their lives and make them seem meaningful again. If you feel this way, it is important to think of things and do things that increase your feelings of power in your life.

1. Look at your positive attributes.
When you are feeling depressed or anxious, most of your thoughts about yourself will be negative. What your mind is telling you is not the truth. Your thinking is inaccurate because of an imbalance of certain neurochemicals in your brain. In order to recover, you must create an equilibrium in your brain chemistry again. How do you do this? Antidepressants can help. But it is just as important, and longer-lasting, to think more positively about yourself.

Use your logical forebrain. The idea that you are only weak is irrational. If that were the case, you wouldn't have come this far in your life. Obviously you have many strengths. You just can't see them right now. According to a recent research study published in *Neuroscience Therapeutics*, it is important to look toward the future instead of dwelling on the past and on your current limitations. Develop skills that help you maintain positive expectations and a positive outlook. Choose to focus on the present and the future instead of the past. Here are some exercises to help you feel stronger, more confident, and more positive about yourself, so you can take charge of your life again. Write down the answers to these exercises in a notebook so that you can reread them and add to them at a future date.

- Make a list of five of your strengths and virtues: (e.g., persistent, critical thinker, loving, courageous, cooperative, work for justice, loyal, responsible, wise, can laugh, creative). At first you may not come up with many strengths. After all, that's not the way your brain is thinking right now. I'll help you by asking you some questions. Do you love your friends and family? Loving others and yourself is the greatest strength you can have in this world. It ultimately creates the peace you have been fighting for in war. Have you helped anyone in your life? Have you ever stayed and faced your problems, or defended someone else by your words or actions, when all you wanted to do was run? This is courage. Have you done well in school, a hobby, at a job?
- Write down any incidents you remember when you displayed these strengths and virtues, whether before, during, or after the war.
- What accomplishments are you proud of in your life? These don't need to be large achievements. Maybe you went to the VA to ask for help, or you have

completed a project you started. Those qualify as accomplishments.
- Write down occasions when you helped someone else, or when you used your strengths and virtues for a purpose greater than your own goals.
- Focus on the things you have the power to change in your life, like your behavior and your thoughts. Write them down.

2. Count your blessings and change your attitude. I'm sure you have heard "count your blessings" before from well-meaning people such as parents, teachers, and religious leaders. But I am asking you to literally list your blessings on paper. I find the easiest way for me to do this exercise is to compare myself to other people in the world. It's amazing how rarely I felt depressed as a psychotherapist who saw eight clients daily, five days a week.

You might remember the country where you were stationed during the war and the people who lived there. What advantages do you have that they didn't have? Did they have freedom of speech and religion? A good education? Health care? Safety? Enough food and decent lodging? My father's family, like many of our immigrant ancestors, fled their home and wealth, leaving everything behind for the privilege of being free. That's what you fought for. Make it real.

Think of yourself as a computer without emotions and look at the situation, knowing all you've experienced. There is hope. Begin to name all the good things you have in your life: a place to live, someone who cares, food, a brain that works.

In general I prefer not to listen to the news too often, but there are times that, in short doses, it helps me to appreciate my blessings. I may feel sorry for myself until I watch a story about earthquake survivors in Haiti who have lost their entire families, homes, and jobs, and struggle just to remain alive and find food and water. Wow! I am blessed.

3. List your ideals and principals. What do you believe in? What gives you purpose and hope? Listen to your voice when you talk about a topic with your friends and family. What topics give you energy? What makes your voice rise and gets you excited? What makes you laugh? You might think you have no purpose now that you are home, but that's not true. Ask yourself, "Why did I enlist? What gave me purpose during the war? Was it supporting and working together with my unit? Helping my country? Creating justice?"

All of these aspirations don't need to change when you come home. Our country and our people need your help right here. There are jobs available in the police force, the FBI, border patrol, firefighting, youth work, and relief in the wake of disasters such as earthquakes, hurricanes, super-storms, floods and fires. If you're unable to get employment in these areas, volunteer your time and cooperate with others who believe in the same ideals that you do. Keep our country safe and free right here at home. We need you.

4. List your goals for the present and the future. What do you want your life to look like in five years? Ten years? What do you want to accomplish during that time? Who would you like to be in five years? Is there someone you admire? What is it you admire in her or him? Do you want to be more like this person? If so, select one area at a time you want to change in yourself, and begin. Again, focus on the things you have the power to change, not on factors out of your control. If you are married or have a long term partner, include her or him in this exercise. What are her or his goals? How can each of you compromise and make the goals comfortable for both of you?

5. List your priorities. Do you know what your priorities are? Many people think they do. But are they being honest? There is one sure way to find out. Check your actions. Are they congruent with what you say or think? For example, you may say your priority is family, yet you rarely have time to spend with your mate or children. You may say your priority is education, but you never check out what the GI Bill can do to help you go back to school. You may say your priority is getting a job, but you don't apply because the position offered is not exactly what you want. Make sure your actions match your true priorities.

6. Organize your life. Make lists of what to do, what to buy, etc., and prioritize them. Researchers are finding that keeping lists can double or even triple your output a day. Plus they will decrease your stress level considerably and eliminate most crises in your life. Plan your week in advance. Place a date beside each item as to when you need to accomplish it. Include bills to pay and appointments to keep. Then go on to the next list. Before you go to bed, make a list of what you need to do the next day, step by step. Prioritize the steps by placing number 1 behind the most urgent one, number 2 behind the next, etc. The next day, strike out each item as you accomplish it. If life intervenes and you cannot get everything done by the date you set, place new dates on them. Reprioritize the list if need be. Be realistic. There is only so much most of us can achieve in a single day or even a week.

7. Solve problems and make decisions. Here are some steps to follow when you have an important decision to make, such as finding a job or returning to school:

- Write down your problems in your notebook, leaving a few pages for each. Give yourself enough space to include what is going on in your life, what you think and feel about various issues, and possible solutions.
- List as many possible solutions as you can think of. Leave some space after each solution. Be as creative as you can, even if you think the answer sounds silly or won't work (e.g., run away from home, live on a desert island, go out and fight). Some ideas will probably make you smile, but often they can be combined with other ideas or trigger thoughts of still more options that might work. Then do your research. Find out the facts. Call friends, businesses, or agencies, and look up data on the Internet. There may be more solutions than you knew existed.
- After each solution, list all the positives and negatives of that plan. If, for instance, you wish to buy stock in a company that you really believe will be profitable,

but you don't have the money and the interest rate on a loan is higher than the yield from your stock, you would probably eliminate this solution. Or if you consider family to be your priority and have been offered a job in Alaska and your family can't come with you, you might turn it down. On the other hand, if your family is willing to relocate or the company is willing to compromise and give you one week out of three at home, you and your spouse may agree to accept the job for a year to see how it works out.

- Go through each solution and place an x in front of each plan you know logically and intuitively won't work for you, and a check in front of each one that might work. Pick your battles. It's okay to say, "That solution may give me the outcome I desire, but the stress it would create in my life is more than I want or can handle at this point."
- Place a "1" after the solution you think will work best, a "2" after the second best, etc. See if you can combine some of the solutions.

8. Do things you succeed at to develop self-confidence.

- Write down all the things that keep you from becoming successful. List your feelings such as fear, shame, guilt, embarrassment, helplessness, and anger. Do you have unrealistic expectations? Or have you made poor choices in the past and are afraid you will make another decision that will have negative consequences?

- Sit comfortably in a chair, or lie down, and do some relaxation exercises such as breathing deeply, stretching, and clearing your mind. (Turn to Step Four for more details about relaxation). When you are relaxed, recall occasions when you felt capable and successful, creating a strong image in your mind of these incidents.
- Maintain focus on your success for long periods of time and the wiring in your brain will actually change. Imagine, imagine, imagine success.
- Now act. Do something you know you can successfully accomplish. Set yourself up for success by doing things you usually do well. If you know you can't hold a note, now is not the time to try singing an aria. Instead, if you are a good writer, why not write an article or a blog for a veterans' site?

9. **Change your body language.** Your mind and body are very closely connected. Within a fraction of a second, your body will show what is going on in your mind, even though you are not aware of either the thought or the change in your body language.

- First of all, become aware of what is happening in your body when you are under stress or you are in a difficult situation. Is your jaw tight or your fist clenched? Are your shoulders slumped and your head bowed? Are you frowning? Or do you glance away and avoid making eye contact with the person beside you? Other people pick up cues from your body language and react accordingly. If they perceive you to be a victim, they will treat you as a victim. If you come across as being angry and possibly violent, they tend to retreat and don't want to be near you. If they see you as powerful and assertive but not aggressive, they will recognize you as a leader and respect you.

- Become aware of your posture as you go about your day and meet challenges. Decide on what image you would like your bearing to portray.
- Practice in front of a mirror. Straighten your back and your shoulders, hold your head up high, swing your arms as you walk, and smile a genuine smile (one that affects your eyes as well as your mouth.) Look straight into someone's eyes, but not so long that you intimidate her or him.
- Next time you meet a challenge, like a job interview, check your body language immediately and change it if you need to, even though you may not feel like it. Act "as if." It will influence both your own and others' opinion of you, as well as your mood.
- Role-play with a family member or friend before you go to a job interview.
- Clean up and dress up. In our culture, dressing in nice, clean clothes usually changes how we look at ourselves and how others see us. Feeling more confident automatically changes your body language. Your clothes and demeanor are particularly important when you are interviewing for a job. If you don't have the money to buy a suit (or whatever clothes are appropriate), visit thrift stores (they are called

"once loved" clothing stores in New Zealand) or the Salvation Army, where you can get great clothes for very little money.

10. **Become future-directed. Take action.** As much as possible, focus on the future, not on the past or on your current limitations. Maintain a positive expectation about the future. Although deciding what you want to do in the future is important, you must take action in order to make your life what you want it to be. Make plans for the present *and* the future. Then make them a reality. Now that you know what your goals are, write down a plan for how to get there. What do you need to do first? Next? If you are married or have a long-term partner, do this exercise together. Is she or he willing to help? In what way(s)?

11. **Be realistic. When you act, you will run into obstacles you didn't expect.** Whether we like it or not, the truth is that we are not in control of everything in our lives. Alcoholics Anonymous (AA) has a prayer that the group repeats at every meeting. It is not religion-specific, but if you believe in a "higher power" than yourself, it can work for you. You may have heard it:

God grant me the Serenity to accept the things I cannot change, Courage to change the things I can, and Wisdom to know the difference.

Substitute your own word for God if you wish. It could be Creator, Higher Power, Allah, Jehovah, Life Force or whatever word you use to symbolize a power greater than yourself, in whom you trust. Write down the prayer and keep

Twenty Steps to Help You Heal

it where you can read it frequently. I keep a copy taped to my dining room hutch.

When you run into an obstacle, make a list of what you can and cannot control. You cannot control nature, such as the weather, disease, or natural disasters. You cannot control what other people think, say, or do. All you really can control is what **you** think, say, and do, and what meanings you attach to an event. Sometimes you can barely control those.

When you list the things you can control, see what you can change and work on those. But even those changes may not always alter the outcome, because you are not in control of how others respond or what happens in the larger world. I remember a time when I was asked to join an AIDS project in Africa. After hesitating, I finally came to the conclusion it was something I needed to do. The day after I said, "yes" happened to be 9/11/01. In the aftermath of the terrorist attacks, all the money from overseas needed to move the project forward was frozen.

Any twelve-step program includes the adage, "Let go and let God," meaning to release control and turn the problem over to God as you understand her/him/it. People often ask, "What does it mean to let go? Am I not supposed to try to change things?" No, that's not what is meant by that statement. To let go means you have done all the things you can to change what is happening in your life, but they haven't worked. You are becoming frustrated and trying harder and harder, but that approach still doesn't work. It's time to let go and turn the problem over to a greater power than yourself.

For example, imagine you have a sick child and you have taken him to the doctor and to a specialist. You've tried every drug and holistic medication available. You've prayed, begging continuously for the child's health to be restored, with no results. It is now time to admit you can't make him well, and that you must let go. It is time to allow and trust your higher power to take charge, regardless of what happens. Often you will come across information serendipitously that can help you.

Letting go is not an easy task, but it brings peace and acceptance into your life.

12. List what you have learned from your experience. How have you grown? Can you see a silver lining in the cloud? Did the trauma help you or save you somehow? Maybe you learned something about life or how to cope with it that will always be of value to you. Maybe your beliefs and attitudes have changed. Maybe you have developed more empathy for others. Maybe you feel closer to your family than you ever did before the trauma. Instead of seeing only the negative consequences of the trauma, you can choose to look at positive ones as well.

When David was shot in Iraq, he felt devastated. Although the medical team at the army hospital saved his life, he took months to recover and was never able to run again. But here is the silver lining: during the initial surgery after his injury, the doctors found that David had developed a serious heart problem since his enlistment. They immediately performed a triple bypass. The doctor told him that if he had continued on active duty, he might well have suffered a heart attack. Ultimately the injury may have saved his life.

STEP FOUR:
Learn to relax.

Many of your physical and emotional symptoms of PTS decrease when you relax. Your blood pressure and pulse rate drop, your muscles loosen, and your anxiety lessens. If this does not occur, you may be someone for whom relaxation exercises increase anxiety. Usually this is not the case, but it does happen more frequently among PTSD sufferers. That's okay. For you, relaxing means you are not on alert, ready to act in case of an emergency. So there's a part of you that says, "It's dangerous to relax." Very understandable, since you can't trust anyone or anything during combat. If this is the case, skip the following suggestions for now. If relaxation exercises tend to increase your anxiety, simply exercising and flexing your muscles can help loosen them up and make you feel calm.

For those of you who can relax without negative effects, try to practice at least one technique that quickly relaxes your body and reduces your stress. The following exercises are easy and anyone can do them. But like so many things in life, it takes practice, practice, practice.

1. **Do deep-breathing exercises.** When you feel stressed, take time to breathe in and out, deeply and slowly, several times. Breathe in through your nose and out through your mouth, all the way, until you've emptied your lungs. Breathing in through your nose actually cools the amygdala (emotional brain) and reduces its reactivity. Put all your attention onto the rising and falling of your chest. Experience what the breath feels like in your body. Hear it going in and out. You will notice that when you breathe out fully, there is a moment that the muscles in your body relax naturally and completely.

2. **Recognize what makes you relax.** Is it an image, a sound, a smell, a feeling of an object? The answer usually depends on which is the dominant sense (sight, hearing, smell, taste, or touch) that you use to communicate with the world. You may have two senses that both serve you well. Try using the different senses. Look at a picture, listen to your favorite music, smell something you like to smell, eat your favorite food, touch your favorite blanket. After using each sense, check in with how your body feels.

3. **Take a hot shower or bath.** The heat of the water flowing over your body helps your muscles relax. Some people take a couple of showers a day, more to relax than to stay clean. My son used to stand in the shower for twenty minutes each evening to allow himself to relax so he could fall asleep more easily after a hard day at school.

4. Remember a time (or times) in your life when you felt completely relaxed. You were able to relax because you felt safe. Write these memories down in your journal with as much detail as you can. For many of you, this may be a time spent outside, far away from other people. Others might recall sitting next to a stream, listening to a gurgling brook or skipping rocks across a lake. Others will picture themselves indoors, maybe as a child at home with the family, or at Grandma's house, smelling her cooking and eating a piece of apple pie. Others may recall lying in bed, stroking a soft, fuzzy blanket, or playing with a cat or dog. The place or time of your memory does not need to comply with other people's expectations. This is *your* journey.

Close your eyes. Now return to that place and time, imagining it in as much detail as possible. Imagine yourself in that environment, looking around in all directions. What do you see and hear? What do you smell? What do you feel or touch? How old were you when you were there? Allow yourself to fully relax in that place. Some people will fall asleep. That's okay. As a matter of fact, this is an excellent exercise to do if you have difficulty falling asleep.

Relaxing music helps. It is best to use one favorite piece over and over again each time you do these exercises, so that your mind can tie it to your feeling of relaxation.

5. Find a quiet spot where you will not be disturbed. Turn off your phone. If you're able, lie down and make sure you are comfortable. One of my clients used to go to the creek near her house and lie down in the long grass under a willow tree, far away from everyone.

6. Learn to move your mind away from everyday or worrisome thoughts.

- Pretend you are placing all your worries, one by one, onto the cloud floating by overhead, or into a container. Name the worries as you go. Close the container and lock it, then send it away on the clouds or down a stream or river. Watch the cloud or the container float farther and farther away and disappear.
- Another technique that works for some people is to play specific music (usually quiet, soft music) that takes their mind away and helps them relax. You need to experiment with the kind of music that works best for you.
- Some people hold an object that is symbolic of the place or feeling they wish to recall. It is comforting. One veteran carried a medal he had been awarded to remind him of his competence and bravery when life got tough. Others carry a favorite rock, a seashell, or textured object they can touch. One person dabbed a little peppermint oil on his palm to remind him of his years in Idaho, growing up near his parents' peppermint fields. Any object can trigger relaxation if it has a quiet, safe memory attached to it.

7. Do a progressive relaxation exercise as an alternative to imagining a place. After you lie down and send away your worries, begin with your toes and move toward your head. Tense your toes, then tell yourself to relax them. Let them go limp. Then your foot, your calf, your thigh, continuing up your body to your head. Breathe deeply in and out while you do this exercise.

The techniques I've given you have helped many. However, each person is different. Feel free to create your own techniques if these don't work for you. For example, when one of my clients became anxious, he would stop whatever he was doing and do his own relaxation exercise. He would conjure up an image of mountains in his mind and take three deep breaths, and the stress would disappear like magic. When I asked him how he had started this practice, he said, "When I was in 'Nam, a verse I learned as a kid in Sunday school kept coming back to me. I think it was in Psalms: *I will lift up mine eyes unto the hills from whence cometh my help.* So I did that when things got tough. I imagined the hills I grew up with, near our house in Montana, and then I would slowly breathe in that help, and I would know that I'd be okay." In other words, he created his own unique relaxation exercise that worked for him.

After you have done these exercises for a while—at least once daily—your body, mind, and emotions will trigger each other like Pavlov's dogs were triggered by the bell and the food. And so when you become anxious because of something that happened or something you thought, you will be able to take a few deep breaths, imagine your safe place and/or concentrate on your music, and immediately relax, feeling much less anxious, just as my client did. I can attest to you that relaxation works. It's how I was able to continue working with clients who dealt with PTSD for so many years.

STEP FIVE:
BECOME AWARE OF YOURSELF.

SELF-AWARENESS AND SELF-KNOWLEDGE ARE NOW frequently referred to as "mindfulness," though mindfulness has a broader definition that includes contemplation and meditation. (Meditation will be covered later in this book.) Mindfulness is a technique that can be used by virtually anyone to find balance in her or his life.

In this section I define mindfulness as being purposefully attentive to the present, using all your senses and noting your experiences and your responses to them. **To become self-aware and gain self-knowledge, you must practice staying in the here and now.**

It is common for people to be unaware of their bodily sensations, their feelings, and their thoughts. The more trauma you have experienced, the less likely you are to turn your focus inward. So why am I asking you to become aware of yourself? When you learn to recognize your thoughts, emotions, and physical sensations in the moment, you remain in the present and focus on them instead of on your triggers from the past, and therefore you are less reactive. You have more control in your life, which reduces stress and anxiety. You can see the bigger picture of what is important and what is not. This knowledge allows you to develop clearer thinking and concentration, and thus to change behaviors you don't like and that don't work for you anymore.

Awareness is the first step in changing your behavior. For example, maybe you have a habit of exploding when something stressful happens, or you distance yourself from the people you care about, or you go out and get drunk. Maybe you get angry and throw something, or you run away. But you don't know why you do these things, and often not even why you were stressed in the first place. The undesirable action just happens. Many people believe the behavior is automatic and they have no control over it. Actually this is false. Something is occurring in your mind, your feelings, and your body of which you are not aware.

If you are truly interested in changing the behaviors that are not working for you and are causing you pain, if you want to become a more resilient person, you must become aware of what triggers these feelings. You must notice where the feelings lodge in your body, and what you are thinking when they occur. Until you can tap into them at one of these points inside or outside the body, you have little hope of understanding or changing the pattern. Recognizing how you react to a particular situation allows you to make a choice of what to do, instead of lashing out automatically. **Having a choice helps you gain back your control.**

You are not a victim of your feelings, thoughts, and actions. Thoughts will come and go. Feelings will come and go. They are just that: thoughts and feelings. Don't give them so much credence or space in your life. They don't have that much power unless you allow them to take over your life.

You have a choice as to how you will respond, act, and react. You do not need to say out loud everything you think. You do not need to act on every feeling you have. Again, you have a rational forebrain. If you count to ten before acting, or take yourself out of the situation immediately, you allow that part of your brain to engage. Then you can determine logically how you wish to act.

Just pay close attention to yourself.

Here's an easy check-in. Take a couple of minutes a day to get in touch with yourself. Take time alone in a quiet place so you don't get distracted by outside activity and noise. Whether you choose to stand, sit, or lie down, make sure you are comfortable.

1. Check your bodily sensations. Can you feel where your body touches the chair or ground? Are you feeling hot, cold, warm, comfortable? Are you relaxed or tense? If you are tense, in what areas of the body are you holding the tension and tightness? Your muscles will tell you. Are you shaking or perspiring? Is your heart racing? Do you have any pain? If so, where? Are you hungry? Sleepy? Tired? How is your breathing?

2. Check in with all your senses. What are you seeing right now? Describe it clearly. What are you hearing? Is someone playing music, or are the birds chirping? Is someone mowing the lawn? Can you hear cars? Listen to them carefully. What are you touching? Grass? Cloth? What does it feel like on your skin? Is there a taste you can detect in your mouth? Is there a smell you notice in your surroundings? Maybe it's the smell of flowers or newly mown grass, or a pungent odor, or the odor of sweat. The sense of smell triggers emotions more often than the other senses.

3. Check your feelings. People often say that when they close their eyes and focus on their hearts, they can get in touch more easily with their feelings. Ask yourself, "What am I feeling? Am I sad, happy, content, angry, anxious, afraid?" Some people will need to list various feelings and listen to their body after each one to see whether the feeling seems right.

4. Check your thoughts. What are the images and thoughts moving in and out of your conscious mind? Most of the time your feelings follow your thoughts. For example, you see a program on TV about hundreds of people losing jobs. You think, "Will I lose my job? My company isn't doing well financially." Then you begin to worry. Or you smell smoke in the air, which triggers thoughts of your house burning when you were young, making you feel sad and scared. Or you think of a sunny, relaxing day on the beach, and soon you feel happy, relaxed, and content. Some experts say that negative thinking is just a bad habit and can be changed. (For more about thoughts and how to alter them, see Step Seven).

5. Stay in the here and now. Take on a job or project where your mind cannot wander. Grant, an Iraq veteran, came home with constant memories of his year in battle. I asked him how he had survived. He said, "I took a job as a bulldozer operator for a lumber company. It forced me to stay right there. My mind couldn't wander, or else I would have been in big trouble." (Not that I suggest getting a job as dangerous as this. There are other ways to stay in the here and now.) Another veteran I know became a wildlife photographer. He immersed himself in getting the "perfect photo." Not only did he have to remain in the present to do so, but he had a lot of fun. Doing something creative that also stretches your mind is indeed one way to remain happy.

6. Talk to yourself. I imagine you learned at a young age that talking to yourself was a sign of being "weird" or "crazy." Other kids made fun of you. So you learned to shut down the voices in your mind, thus losing the self-awareness you once had. I suggest that you talk to yourself. But this time, you can do it internally or, if you need to speak out loud, do it when you are alone. Pretend you are two different people, and argue with yourself about an issue. Actually, although we are not "split," we have several voices inside us most of the time. When we have a decision to make, two or more sides of ourselves can emerge and discuss or argue with each other. Listen to these voices inside you, or speak out loud. Become aware of the process. If any of you have watched Stephen Colbert on TV, you might have seen his section called "Worthy Opponent." He creates a clip of two "Stephens" (both him) arguing with each other on an issue he wishes to resolve.

Some of you may have heard of a technique called Gestalt Therapy. In very basic terms, it entails talking to yourself, and is a very powerful way of getting in touch with your inner selves. Imagine the part of you, or the organ that is giving you trouble, or the person with whom you are having difficulty, sitting on the chair across from you. (If that's difficult for you to imagine, place an object on the chair, such as a pillow or picture, that symbolizes the other person or part of yourself.) Then talk to that person or part of yourself as though he/she/it were present right now. Ask him, her, or it any questions you wish and write down the answers that first come into your mind. For example, "Who are you? What do you look like? What are you feeling right now? What are you thinking? What is making you so sad or angry?" When you have finished asking questions of this pretend other person, ask yourself, "What do I want or need to say to that person or part of me?" Then tell that part or person what you would like to say.

If you can't get answers to all the questions mentioned in this section, don't be discouraged. Most people have to learn how to become aware of themselves and must practice frequently. As an example, I knew a veteran committed to change who each time he came to my office, would march in, looking much like the officer he had been in the army. He looked in control. One time he sat down and told me that he had just heard of a close friend who had died in battle. He showed little emotion.

I asked him, "What are you feeling as you tell me this?"

He looked puzzled and shook his head. "I don't know. I don't feel anything. Why are you asking?"

"Well, you just told me that a close friend of yours from your unit died in battle. How does that affect you?"

He swallowed hard. "Oh, okay. I guess I'm sad."

"Where in your body are you feeling it?"

He shrugged and tried to change the subject.

"Emotions are very powerful," I said. "I know that part of you doesn't want to get in touch with them, but the PTSD symptoms won't go away if you don't."

He grunted.

"Picture your body. How do you see yourself?"

He suddenly laughed. "I have steam coming out of my nostrils. I want to kill the men who killed him. I am very angry."

"What are you thinking right now?"

"Those bastards." And on and on.

We placed the "pretend steaming" person on a chair and dialogued with him. You can do this in a journal as well. Write out both sides of the conversation, like dialogue in a play.

You don't have to start immediately by becoming aware of difficult feelings, as this veteran did. Instead, when you go to a restaurant, look around the room and ask yourself which booth would make you feel most relaxed. Test it out. Then try another one. Feel what feels wrong or good in your body. Do the same when you check out the menu.

The sensations in your body will help you make decisions. Some people think that your body or intuition will always lead you right. Often your intuition does help guide you, but I haven't found that it is right every time. Maybe that means most of us aren't good enough at listening to our bodies to get it right. I don't know.

I suggest that, before you make any important decision in your life, you use a healthy dose of brain power and logic as well. Sometimes your body hums with your desires instead of what is good for you. Learn as much as you can about a subject first. Check your priorities. Write down the positives and negatives of each decision. Read Step Three for exercises on decision making and problem solving. Then ask your body what it's trying to tell you.

My husband and I had some money to invest, and we began to explore different options. Friends we trusted asked us to join them in a "sure" investment deal. That should have been our first warning. It was an innovative idea, but there was little information about the area available for us to check. So we decided to ask our intuition about what was best. The adventure sounded right for us at the time, and the possibilities seemed limitless. We jumped without looking squarely at the risk. In the long run we lost our investment. Intuition was not enough.

If you find something you wish to invest in—time, energy, or money—do it knowing clearly what your potential positive outcomes and risks might be. Of course, there are no sure outcomes, but you can mitigate risks by playing it smart.

7. Change your behaviors. When you are fully aware of your physical sensations, your feelings, and your thoughts, it is time to change your behavior to what you wish it to be. Start by running a film in your mind that shows you acting appropriately when something sets you off. Replay this image many times a day. However, you may still make mistakes when an actual event happens that triggers your habitual response, even when you know better. Don't be too hard on yourself. You are human. You can't go from grade three to grade eight in one jump. It's all about learning and practicing.

STEP SIX:

CHECK WITH A DOCTOR TO SEE WHETHER MEDICATIONS CAN HELP

IN MOST CASES WHERE SYMPTOMS are severe, I believe in working on all aspects of a problem at once— emotional, mental, spiritual, and physical—in order to alleviate the severity of symptoms, so people can return to some degree of functioning. If you need relief immediately, it is clear from research that a combination of psychotherapy and medication works more rapidly and effectively than either approach alone. There are many medications that can help you cope with PTS and PTSD. New ones are constantly being discovered. If you are not on any medication at present but you have severe symptoms of PTS, consult your doctor or a psychiatrist at the VA. Medications along with therapy can help you stabilize.

Remember, if you use medication without counseling or without working on steps such as the ones given in this book, your symptoms will decrease only as long as you use the medication. Nothing else changes. You learn no new ways of thinking or coping with stressful events.

Discuss the possibility of using medications with your doctor and your counselor. You will want to be cautious about the length of time you are on medications, especially because some are addicting, but never go off them without consulting your doctor. As a word of warning, it is always advisable to check out any medication for negative side effects that can create more problems than the original symptoms.

This section will be fairly brief, because I am not a medical doctor and do not pretend to know what medications you need and I certainly do not recommend any of these. I merely list a few options that doctors have prescribed to veterans I have talked to. I mainly mention the names of the patented drugs that you will hear or read about, but in many cases there are generic drugs as well. Your doctor will prescribe drugs according to your symptoms.

If you are depressed, doctors most often order the latest antidepressants, selective serotonin reuptake inhibitors (SSRI's), such as Prozac, Zoloft, and Lexapro. Sometimes, depending on your situation, they will prescribe older medications called tricyclics, such as Imipramine. Normally it takes about three weeks for antidepressants to work effectively. Sometimes you may take a drug that doesn't seem to work, and your doctor may need to switch to another one before you find the right one. Also, don't forget that if you decide to discontinue an antidepressant, you cannot suddenly stop your medication. If you do, you may become even more depressed. You must reduce the dosage slowly, under the advice of a physician.

If you suffer from nightmares, Minipress (generic name: Prazosin), a blood pressure medication, is one of the drugs frequently prescribed. Prazosin makes people less sensitive to adrenalin and reduces nightmares. You may also be given beta blockers. These are heart medications that reduce hyper-arousal and block the effects of adrenalin. Anti-anxiety medication, such as Ativan, Klonopin, and Xanax, work for severe anxiety, but are used with caution because they can be addicting.

An antibiotic, D-cycloserine, is now used to treat fears. It enhances fear extinction, especially when used with Prolonged Exposure Therapy (PET). (I will discuss PET in Step Eleven.) If you have problems sleeping, there are several drugs your physician can prescribe. Newer drugs such as Ambien usually do not leave you feeling "hung over" in the morning. For veterans with co-occurring disorders such as bipolar disorder, mood stabilizers can help. For those who have been physically injured in war and find themselves in intense pain a great deal of the time, pain killers such as OxyCoton or Hydrocodone are frequently prescribed.

Different medications work more effectively for some people than others. It may be necessary to try several drugs before your doctor finds the right combination that works for you. Hang in there and don't give up.

There are many drugs for particular symptoms, but so far, none that will modify or erase distressing memories. With the rapid increase of research being conducted on the brain and memory at present, scientists are now on the verge of discovering a solution. The age of memory treatment is here.

Although still not approved for PTSD, two promising drugs that are currently undergoing research may be of interest to you. As mentioned earlier, during a freeze, fight, or flight response, adrenaline sears vivid emotional memories of trauma into the brain with the help of the amygdala. Researchers have recently discovered that a low dose of Proprananol, a blood pressure medication and beta blocker, reduces activity in the amygdala and subdues the freeze, fight, or flight response. Users of Proprananol do not forget the memory, but are actively able to redesign and reconsolidate it. The drug strips away the terror of the trauma while leaving the facts behind, and has been found to be most useful shortly after the trauma has occurred. A McGill University research group collaborating with Harvard psychiatrist Roger Pitman found that after several treatments with Proprananol, PTSD symptoms declined by half and stayed that way even after six months.

At present the U.S. Army has designated $6.7 million to research drugs that go beyond Proprananol. Studies are also being conducted with 3,4-methylenedioxy-N-methyl-amphetamine (MDMA), the active ingredient of the street drug Ecstasy. As does Proprananol, MDMA tames the brain's fear center, the amygdala, allowing PTSD survivors to confront bad memories as necessary without a great deal of fear. They still feel some fear, but trust themselves to go past it. The drugs act similarly to anti-anxiety medications, but without the sedative effects. The patient is free of pain. Michael Mithoefer, a psychiatrist in South Carolina, has found that seventeen out of twenty subjects in his small pilot study no longer met the criteria for PTSD after two or three sessions with MDMA. The drug is still experimental, and possible side effects have not yet been established.

As research continues into memory, neurobiologists have found that certain chemicals in the memory process, when given in high doses, can literally blank out specific memories in animals as the memories are being recalled. They have also discovered ways of eliminating whole categories of memories. The military has invested considerable money to research these chemicals, but their approval for use in humans is probably still some time away.

For most people, this selective memory erasure sounds terrifying. What if the medication doesn't work as scientists think it will, and instead wipes out *all* memories? Yet in spite of the risks, according to researchers, there are people "standing in line" who wish to be research subjects. Many of them are rape survivors.

At present, a third of all PTSD survivors do not recover completely, but the future is promising for severely traumatized persons.

STEP SEVEN:
Change your thinking.

Though separating the emotions, mind, body, and spirit is not possible in reality, I have done so for the purpose of listing steps as logically as I can. So bear with me if some of the next sections overlap somewhat.

Along with Step Eleven, where I describe Prolonged Exposure Therapy (PET), Step Seven is known to be the most effective way to help you recover from severe stress after a trauma. Research shows that these two steps used together are up to 95% effective in treating PTS. But these are not easy steps to do, and many people stop practicing them before they see lasting results. So stick with them. I am confident that if you change your thinking, you will change your life.

When I speak of the mind, I am talking both of that which is conscious and known to you and that which is unconscious and unknown to you. Except for reflexes and instincts, such as the freeze, fight, or flight survival response that literally can save your life (and probably did in combat), most psychologists and scientists now believe that your unconscious and/or conscious thoughts actually occur just prior to your emotions, not the other way around.

With practice you can observe your thoughts and learn to change them, thereby changing your emotions. When you modify your thoughts about a situation, you alter your stress level and your depression. Negative thinking increases your stress and depression; positive thinking decreases it.

Does thinking about something actually attract to you what you want or don't want, as some authors now claim? I really don't know. But I do know from experience that thoughts change our happiness factor and our resilience. They change our outlook on life. They make us aware of our options. Even so, it is still up to us to make decisions and take actions.

Unconscious, implicit beliefs lead to thoughts, then to emotions, and then to actions. Without actions, your dreams will not become reality. One of my clients, who felt very lost when he returned from the war, came up with a plan for a business. He was excited about what he was going to do and thought about it constantly. But he never took any action. I imagine you know how the story ended.

Though negative thinking is partly genetic, you have programmed negative thoughts about yourself into your mind over many years. (If you didn't, psychologists would probably call you a narcissist.) Maybe people in your past reminded you, or at least implied, that you were "stupid" or that you were a "failure," and you have incorporated those voices into your thinking.

I have mentioned the word "perception" in Part One. Your perception of yourself, of others, and of events is the key to your success and happiness. What is your perception of yourself? Those programmed voices from the past determine how you see yourself, often on an unconscious level. Occasionally your inner voices tell you that you are so terrific, you don't need to change. That is rare. Usually they say phrases like, "I can't do it," "I'm bad," "I have no control," "Terrible things can happen to me and I won't see them coming," or "I have to be alert all the time to be prepared." Interestingly, research indicates that chronic anxiety is more common among people whose family history fosters the perception that aversive events are unpredictable and uncontrollable.

A highly effective form of treatment for reducing and managing PTS is called Cognitive Therapy. Briefly, Cognitive Therapy teaches you how to change your perception and your thoughts in order to control anxiety and depression. Treatment gains have been shown to be long-lasting.

Many people think they have no control over their thoughts. Wrong. Your mind is malleable, and what you think is knowable and therefore largely in your control. That's comforting. Believing you have no control in your life causes much more stress. You must become aware of your thoughts or you can't change them. For example, you may feel sadness, guilt, and maybe anger. However, you are not aware of what you were thinking. All you understand is the emotion, and sometimes not even that. But you can learn. You are no longer at war, and it's time to move on, to gain some control over your emotions and thoughts so you can live a normal life at home and reintegrate into society.

HOW CAN YOU CHANGE YOUR THOUGHTS?
Thoughts are so automatic that they run like a continuous CD on a computer. When I asked my clients what they were thinking just prior to the flashback, fear, or anger, the majority did not know. Most of them looked puzzled and said, "I'm not thinking anything. It just happens. My anger is just suddenly there."

If you aren't aware of what you are thinking, you are not alone. Most people don't know what their unconscious thoughts are, and they frequently have no idea what to do about their feelings. Many people don't even know what they are feeling. Someone says to you, "You look angry. What's going on?" and you say, "What are you talking about? I'm not angry." The truth is that you were thinking about something that triggered the anger, but both the thought and the feeling were unconscious.

I hate to admit that I used to be a perfectionist. (Well, according to some people who know me, I still am— just a bit, of course.) When I first decided to change my thinking, I began to listen to the messages my mind was giving me. After a while, I realized that several times a day, someone inside my mind kept saying, "It doesn't matter how hard you try, you'll never do it well enough." The voice didn't say, "You're a terrible, no-good louse," but that regardless of what I did, I'd never figure out how to get it right, even though I had no way of knowing what the word *right* meant. I knew one thing. How could I possibly succeed if that's what I was telling myself over and over again? Wow! Now I had a choice.

It became a challenge for me to become aware of what I was thinking. So I did what I thought of as a research experiment. After I felt any emotion, negative or positive, I stopped and asked myself, "What am I thinking?" After a while, that little voice inside began to answer. When I experienced joy, the inner voice spoke of positive things I had accomplished, or of happy memories from my past, or of things or people I loved. When I was sad, fearful, or angry, it spoke of something negative, like a loss, a difficult memory, or a frightening event that had happened or might happen in the future. Thus I felt anxious and depressed.

Where do these voices come from? Usually they come from the past, from family, teachers, friends, work, the culture at large. Where had I learned to believe that I wasn't good enough? My parents and many of the people around me were perfectionists. Without meaning to, they gave me the impression I had to be perfect, whatever that meant. However, deep inside I knew I could never achieve that perfection. One of my clients said she remembered the exact day as a child when she finally accepted her parents' messages that she was an evil child. She spent time and a lot of energy changing those messages, and is now a physicist at a national research laboratory.

Figuring out where the messages came from is enlightening, but what is more important is to understand that your mind has accepted those messages and is feeding them back to you daily, at numerous times and in numerous ways. You are not different or weak for having these thoughts. Everyone has them.

On the other hand, some realistic expectations and self-judgment are positive. If a student gets an F on her paper and the professor, teacher, or parent gives her a gold star or other reward, she probably won't try to improve. But if they say, "You are intelligent, but you really don't know the subject well enough to pass this course and you'll need to get a tutor to catch up," the student will have higher expectations of herself and probably achieve more in life.

Now that the data about our youngest generation—often called the "self-esteem generation"— is coming in, we are finding that many of those kids have little motivation to change, strive to do better, work hard, or even compete with themselves or others. Accustomed to receiving praise for merely existing, they have nothing to achieve. Some think they are owed rewards and that everything should be given to them. They believe they can do whatever they feel like and they'll still "pass the grade" without having to work for it. Then when they get out into the real world, they have a tough time adjusting to the expectations of an employer or spouse.

If you are honest and realistic with yourself, you can learn a great deal from adversity. You can grow stronger. You can handle more setbacks and cope better with life's ups and downs.

1. **Become aware of your thoughts:** Here are a few ways to become aware of your thoughts.

- **Journal in a free flow way, without thinking about what you are writing.** Then read it back to yourself, out loud. Several times a day, ask yourself what you are thinking at that moment. A good time to practice this is when you have reacted to a problem in a way you didn't consciously want to and have no idea why you did so, or when you experience any strong feeling. Ask yourself, "What am I thinking?" Don't just say, "I don't know." Tell your mind it has permission to answer without being judged for the answer.

- **Pretend you are talking to your mind.** Imagine your mind in any way that comes to you. A lot of people envision their mind as another person whom they can ask a question. Then talk to your mind, ask it questions, and listen to its answers. Crazy? Maybe, but your mind is magnificent and powerful, and holds the answers inside. This technique has worked for many people in my practice.
- **Use free association.** Freud discovered this technique many years ago, and it still works well. In free association, you say a word or think of an incident, and whatever word or image first comes into your mind is what the unconscious mind is associating with that word or incident. Make a list of at least four associations. For example: War—gunpowder—explosions—screams—death. Free association may help you dig down to what is really bothering you.
- **Listen to your body.** Some people wonder how to know for sure that they have received the right answer when using these techniques. You won't always know, but most of the time, the words or images that surface fit the situation. Your mind and body are so closely related that the body will respond almost instantaneously to your thoughts. Either it will tense up and your heart will start racing, or it will relax and slow

down. Some people say, "It just feels right." My husband knows when he is on the right track when tears come to his eyes. If you are not aware of what you are thinking or feeling, pay attention to your body, which will respond moments after your thoughts.

Notice when and where your muscles tense. Are you gritting your teeth? Are you tapping your foot? Ask yourself, "Why am I tapping my foot? What am I feeling?" You may find that usually you tap your foot when you are anxious, grit your teeth when you are angry, and smile when you are happy. Then ask yourself, "What was I thinking that brought on that body response?"

2. Change your thoughts and reprogram your brain.

Change your thoughts, change your feelings. Changing your thinking has been found to be as useful for treating depression as chemical antidepressants, although it takes longer to retrain your brain than to take a medication. However, as long as you practice this step, the effect remains. Your mind is literal, and it will believe what you tell it, if the thought is repeated often enough. When you change your thinking about an event or trauma, your perception of it also changes. Have you ever heard the phrase, "Well, it all depends on how you look at it?" That's what I mean. Here are several ways to change your thinking:

- **Educate yourself about PTS and PTSD** so that you know the facts, not the myths and rumors. Read Part One of this book and any other reliable resource.

- **Read positive literature.** Depending on your preference, read inspirational stories and positive self-help books (*Feeling Good* by David Burns is a classic in the field), or spiritual literature, such as the Bible or other religious books. Make sure the books you choose induce a hopeful feeling inside you and don't increase your fears, depression, and hopelessness. (No help needed in that department. You are already doing that all by yourself.)
- **Make positive statements or affirmations.** Once you become aware of your thoughts, it is time to do something about them. As I said earlier, the mind is malleable and literal, and it will believe what it is told over and over again. That's how a politician can convince you of what he wants you to believe. Just repeat the lie or half truth (or whatever you prefer to call it) often enough, in an authoritative way and your mind says, "Yes." Try it. Some books tell you to merely rephrase the thought into the opposite positive response and repeat it over and over. Each time you hear yourself saying something negative to others or to yourself, turn it around. For example, if you hear yourself saying or thinking, "I am stupid and will never master these techniques," switch to "I choose to change my thoughts. I am wise, and my mind learns easily."

Dr. Mark William Cochran, a military veteran, chiropractor, and speaker, says in his book *Oby's Wisdom: A Caveman's Simple Guide to Holistic Health and Wellness*, "Know that affirmations are not an accurate description of what is going on for you now.

It is not the reality you desire. Your affirmations are statements to affirm the truth that you have decided to create for yourself."

- **Change your story.** What is the internal story you have created about yourself? About having PTS or PTSD? Dr. Cochran frequently speaks about how he dealt with a severe arthritic condition he developed while in the Marines, and how he regained his health to the point that he was able to run a marathon. He says that the single biggest factor in recovering his health was changing his story about himself.

  For years he held the identity of a guy with a debilitating and crippling disease, even though he was doing everything he could to fight the disease. Ultimately he realized that his perspective was keeping him locked into the disease. **He shifted his focus from fighting to thriving.** Rather than let himself be driven by the disease, he recognized that he had an amazing power within himself to heal. We all do. His thoughts and actions shifted, and today he does everything he can to allow his internal healing wisdom to work to its maximum potential.

- **Choose your focus.** Where is your focus? Focus on greatness, not on your limiting beliefs. When negative thoughts occur, tell your mind that you will not focus on them. Focus on aliveness, energy, and love, and be grateful for your life. A couple of years ago, doctors thought my husband, whom I love very much, would not recover from an illness. As I sat beside his hospital bed, I checked in on my thoughts several times a day.

I would tell myself, "Anna, you have a choice as to what you focus on in your thoughts at this moment. You have a choice as to how you will respond to this situation." Sometimes I could refocus on the present or on the positive and be thankful he was still alive, or I could call a friend for support. Other times, I remained in my negative thoughts. But at least I knew I had made that choice, and at any moment I could choose differently.

- **Talk to yourself.** As you become more aware of negative thoughts and beliefs that are not working for you, talk to yourself. Usually the thoughts and beliefs come from the past and are not really true, so convince your mind that these thoughts have little to do with you now. Use words such as, "That really isn't true. I am a capable person. Just because I blew it this time doesn't mean much. I have been successful in many ways in my life." Then name the times you've been successful.

- **Watch a positive, inspirational, or funny movie or listen to music that calms you.** Nature sounds, meditation CDs, guitar music, and other soft music usually calm your mind. Very loud music, such as hard rock, can be jarring and make you feel more depressed. Don't see movies or play songs that you know tend to make you feel depressed or agitated. For each individual, this will be different. For example, I go into an immediate funk listening to country music songs about all the spurned lovers who would rather die than go on without their sweethearts.

- **Use a mantra.** Another way to change your thoughts is to repeat a calming word or phrase over and over to yourself. Find a positive phrase that calms and comforts you such as, "Love will overcome." Some people use vocalizations such as "Ohm." Some people in twelve-step programs repeat the Serenity Prayer many times a day (see Step Ten). This prayer is not religion-specific. Some people use verses from their favorite religious text that reassure them and bolster their beliefs.

  Another classic book, *The Power of Positive Thinking* by Norman Vincent Peale, is a resource in which several of my Christian clients have found mantras. In it, Peale suggests repeating portions of positive Bible verses. Two verses he mentions are, "I can do all things through Christ who strengthens me," and "If you have faith as small as a mustard seed, you can remove mountains."

- **Reframe your thoughts.** Change the meaning that an event or experience holds for you. Look at a situation from a different angle. You don't need to deny reality, but you do have a choice as to where you want your mind to spend most of its time. You can shine a flashlight on the problem or the solution, on the positive or the negative side of the issue. The positive is no less true than the negative, just located at the other end of the spectrum called life. It must, however, ring true, at least to some extent.

People have the option to view negative experiences as opportunities to learn from and become better people. They might say, "This trauma has given me an opportunity to understand how other people feel in similar situations." They can ask themselves, "What have I learned from this? How can I gain strength from adversity? How can I remain optimistic and hopeful in this situation?" They can choose to focus on the silver lining in the cloud, rather than on the darkness. As they reframe their thoughts, they grow and become stronger.

3. Practice Rational Emotive Behavior Therapy. For some people, affirmations feel like lies and veer too far from their beliefs to accept. They think, "This is not logical. I'm not safe. Anything could happen at any time. I have no control. I am just lying to myself when I come up with these unrealistic, positive ways of thinking about the trauma and myself." If this is how you feel, Rational Emotive Behavior Therapy might be for you.

In 1955 Dr. Albert Ellis developed Rational Emotive Behavior Therapy (REBT) as a realistic and more "honest" therapeutic technique to work with thoughts. This technique will help you change your thinking slowly and rationally, so that you can believe what you are saying to yourself. The technique is quite simple. All you will need is a sheet of paper and a pen:

- **Divide your paper into three columns.**

- **After a stressful incident, monitor your thoughts and write them down in the first column.** It takes practice, but need take only a few minutes a day. What are your current beliefs? The trauma may well have changed them. Perhaps you used to believe you were safe, that you could trust people, and that you were in control of your life, but not anymore. If you are not aware of your thoughts, stop yourself each time you experience a strong feeling. If anger is your main issue, notice the anger and stop. Ask yourself, "What am I thinking?" Or "What am I angry about?" Allow an answer to come to you. Accept whatever first enters your mind. Usually it is correct. For example, a common thought for people with PTS is, "I have no control. Things will never change. I can't handle this anymore." Maybe you were thinking about something that happened in the war. Maybe you were thinking, "Nobody at home ever understands me. This always happens." Then look at what triggered the thought. It can be something very small, such as your mate frowning at you, or your son rebelling against you.

Once you are aware of your physical sensations, your automatic beliefs and thoughts, and your feelings, write them down in the first column. Usually the negative thoughts are "always" and "never" thoughts. "This will never change." Or you might be creating catastrophes in your mind, or maybe you are over-generalizing, thinking that "everyone" is not to be trusted, instead of just the one person who hurt you. Some people call this "stinking thinking."

After a war, veterans often feel guilt and shame. They think, "I shouldn't be the one who's alive. If only I had done 'it' differently, one of my troop members would not have died. I'm ashamed of myself. I didn't do my best." Or, "Everything is going to hell. Nobody loves me. The world is a terrible place." Or, "I'll never get a job. I might as well give up."

When you do this exercise, also notice your happy and contented thoughts. "I love sitting here looking out at the mountains with no gunfire nearby." Or, "It's so nice to connect with my son." Or, "Gosh that spaghetti tastes good." This will give you an idea of what makes you happy to be home.

- **Now ask yourself, "How true are these thoughts?"** Use the second column to write down what is logically true. Whenever you find yourself saying or thinking words such as "always" and "never," check yourself. Is that really true? Is it true things will never change? Are you sure? How do you know? Think of times things have changed for you. Maybe you say to yourself, "I can't handle it anymore. I'm too weak." In reality, you've handled it until now and survived. Sure, all humans have weaknesses, but what are the strengths you have that have helped you survive life thus far? What can you do to get help? Name specific strengths and instances when you have come through a

stressful situation. Remember what you did and what worked for you.
- **Rewrite your thoughts so they are rational.** In the third column, rewrite what is really true. Say, "My thoughts at the time were not true, but this is what is really true. There are times I feel weak, like right now, but there have been many times when I've been strong." List a few past incidents to remind you.
- **Practice. Practice. Practice.** You may be getting tired of this word, but it's the best way to continue your recovery and make it long-lasting. Soon you'll be able to complete the exercise in your mind without writing it down, though it is still good to write it down so you can review it whenever you need to.
- **Now determine the behavior you wish to change and how you wish to go about it.** Check Step Eight for ideas on how to do this.
- **Take action.**

STEP EIGHT:
Change unwanted behaviors

CHANGE IS DIFFICULT FOR HUMANS. We gravitate toward what is familiar and feels safe. That's the way our brain works, and old habits die slowly. Just thinking differently about something is great, but in order to be in control of your life again, you must change your actions as well. We are not in control of many things outside ourselves, but most of the time we are in control of our own behaviors (actions and reactions).

Did you know that long-lasting change is most likely to occur during a crisis like the one you may be undergoing at present? People will do almost anything to get rid of physical and/or emotional pain. But depending on people's tolerance levels, it may take extraordinary pain and discomfort to motivate them to grow and change. You may have heard the saying, "The pain must outweigh the gain you receive from a negative behavior." I don't believe it is necessary to "hit bottom" before you change, but I do know that pain is one of the greatest motivators in the world. On the other hand, sometimes the motivator can be something positive, such as love, money, relationships, or happiness.

The motivation to change a behavior starts with a strong feeling. Whenever you react or act in response to a strong feeling, there will be consequences, either positive or negative. When you are hungry, you eat. When you are lonely, you visit a friend. When you are in love, you struggle to be with that person. When you believe someone wants to harm you or someone you love, you run or fight. When you lose your job and your spouse or partner threatens to leave, you stop drinking. First the feeling, then the action.

Here are some ideas to help you change your behavior:

1. **Make a list of behaviors you would like to change.** Ask yourself, "Why do I wish to change these behaviors? What negative consequences am I experiencing because of these behaviors?" Write the consequences below each behavior, so that you can read them several times when you are tempted to forget about the changes you wish to make.

2. **Prioritize the list.** What behavior is causing you the most difficulty? Are you drinking too much or doing drugs, and therefore you have lost your job? Are you violent, and therefore your wife is threatening to leave? Write these behaviors in order of the physical or emotional pain they cause you.

3. **Ask yourself, what would create the greatest gain in your life if you changed that behavior?** Ask yourself, "What is most important to me? My family? A job?" Sometimes the greatest pain and the greatest gain come from the same behavior (but not always).

4. Intentionally choose one behavior on the list you wish to change immediately. I imagine you want to change all of them at once, but that would be setting yourself up for failure. Take one behavior at a time. It may not be the hardest behavior to change. Sometimes it is better to choose an easier, less consequential one to begin with, so that you can experience a quick success to boost your confidence.

5. Identify the feeling that best motivates you to change a specific behavior. Allow yourself to feel that feeling completely (e.g., fear of losing your partner and kids). Bring to mind various events that trigger that feeling. Then cultivate the ability to remember and shift into that state at will. This will motivate you to continue on your new path. For example, one of my clients found himself eating more and more and gaining weight because of his frustration at not finding a job. Then he met a friend he had not seen for some time who had gained a lot more weight than he had.

His friend had a great deal of difficulty getting up the stairs and even walking to his car. As a soldier, my client had thrived on his agility. The terror of losing the ability to move at will motivated him to exercise to relieve stress, instead of eating. Every time he wanted to eat when stressed, he held the image of his friend in his mind and felt the fear of becoming helpless. When he did this, the need to overeat would vanish for the time being.

Also remember occasions when you distinctly experienced the feelings you want to feel, such as pride, joy, and relaxation. Positive feelings are as effective as negative ones for motivating behavioral changes. Practice shifting into good feelings, like the veteran who wanted to stop overeating. He told me how proud he felt of himself when he said no to a donut his boss had offered him. That feeling of pride was as effective in motivating him to eat properly as was his fear of becoming disabled.

6. Look at your behavior and ask yourself how you are benefitting from it. What have you gained from continuing the behavior that outweighs the pain it causes? Maybe you get more attention. Maybe lashing out releases your anger and makes you feel more powerful again. Maybe your addiction has eased your physical and emotional pain, at least for short periods, so you feel you can continue living. (Because drugs stimulate the pleasure center in your brain and increase the dopamine level, sobriety is even harder to maintain than other behavior changes.)

7. Are you motivated enough to actually carry out long-term behavioral changes? Ask yourself these questions to determine the answer:

- What will happen if you continue as you have been? Might your loved one leave?
- How would you feel if that happened? Do you really, really want him or her to stay?
- What would have to happen to make life so painful that you would change your behavior to avoid it?
- What reward would make the change worthwhile?
- Is there a different, more positive behavior that will still give you the rewards you crave?

8. Consider not only this week, but the years to come. Now set up a plan as to how you will go about making the changes. What circumstances make it easiest for you to change? Do you need to find a new job or go back to school so you can get the job you would love?

9. If you feel frozen in place, literally get moving again. You will begin to believe you can take control of your life when you get moving. Go for walks and move your legs and arms. When one man I worked with began spending an hour a day walking in the mall, his life began to move forward again. When you exercise your muscles, beneficial chemicals are released. Breathe deeply and slowly, stand up straight, roll back your shoulders, hold up your head and smile, and you will begin to feel more in control and competent. Act "as if."

Your body language can change your mood. Cesar Millan, television's "Dog Whisperer," gives some great examples involving dogs. When a dog comes to him depressed, with its tail between its legs, Milan literally lifts the tail up. Soon the dog re-engages in life again, wagging its tail.

10. Use your imagination. When you get anxious about the trauma, you are usually feeling unsafe. You believe you have little or no control over the situation and the future. Think back to a time you felt safe. Create a safe place to go to in your mind, and strengthen the image to the point you can go there at will whenever you feel threatened. Use all five senses.

For one person, "safety" might mean going into the woods alone, as a child. In play therapy, most people see humans as most dangerous, animals less so, and vegetation as least dangerous.

However, if your trauma took place in nature, you may see the outdoors as a dangerous place. In that case, choose a different image. One woman who had lost everything in a tornado felt safe only when she imagined herself in the arms of her mother. She had learned to trust her implicitly as a child.

STEP NINE:

Work with your emotions ("energy in motion").

The Healing Wall, Part III
by Patrick Overton, Vietnam veteran

III.
*I was becoming part of the Wall, or the Wall part of me.
The more I tried to move away, the more I couldn't move.
It began to pull out of me
emotions I had not felt since I was there,
since that first moment I saw and knew
I had been part of someone's death-
reliving the moment of lost innocence,
remembering the emptiness,
feeling again, the sickness in my heart
I had kept numb for years.
That is when the first tear came, and then a second,
followed by more-
slow tears, warm tears from down deep inside the hole of me.
I became a prisoner of the Wall, captive by its silent,
vigilant, roll call of death.*

To help you navigate your painful emotions, I suggest you become familiar with the earlier steps and become stable first, before approaching this step. Practice ways to stabilize yourself before you deal with your feelings, if possible. Consider seeing a therapist who can direct and support you through this process safely. In all cases I recommend you arrange to have someone whom you trust available if you need her or him.

What are emotions? They are merely "energy in motion" in your body. But sometimes they can be very powerful, especially if repressed for some time. Often when people think of the word "emotion," their bodies clutch. When they think of a trauma, pain floods their bodies, and they run as far and as fast as they can in the opposite direction.

Is it always essential to remember your past trauma and deal with the emotions it triggers? Not always. For some people, remembering makes them less functional, at least for a while. And for some people, their emotions seem overwhelming, and they are terrified of losing control of themselves. You will need to be the one to decide if or when you wish to explore your feelings more deeply.

Although I advise not delving into your emotions and traumatic memories until you have stabilized and learned how to change your thinking, following this advice is not always feasible. Some of you have no choice. Your memories and emotions come to greet you without your permission. You come back from the war and your brain won't allow you to wait to deal with your emotions, even if you would like to. In this case trying to stop them merely makes your symptoms worse.

Many of you have shut down or cut off your emotions during the war. To help you act quickly and stay on high alert during a crisis, your body has a wonderful way of numbing out or dissociating so that you can function. Your brain automatically shuts down the feelings you would not otherwise have been able to handle. The problem is that, for most people, the emotions return sooner or later after the crisis is over. Side stepping them may work for a while, but not forever.

The power your past trauma holds over you often depends on your avoiding it. According to Dr. Gabor Maté in *When the Body Says No*, in order to be healthy physically, mentally, and emotionally, the energy needs to flow instead of remaining stuck in the body. Research now indicates that those who can release their anger live on average two years longer than those who cannot. But you must learn to release your negative emotions in a healthy way so you don't hurt yourself or someone else.

Emotions such as grief, guilt, and anxiety can be very painful, but when you stop them from flowing, other emotions such as joy and happiness usually stop flowing as well. This energy stoppage is what causes the numbness many people feel after a trauma.

In most cases, when the trauma-induced emotions return, you need to deal with them and release them in order to regain normal functioning. The process reminds me of heating water in a pressure cooker. If you close the lid, it may take a little time for the steam to build in the container, but nature determines that the cooker will inevitably explode. Right before it does, you have a choice: to turn off the burner and lift the lid at least a little so the steam can slowly escape, or to watch the pot blow up and cause serious damage. In the case of bottled-up emotions, you may try to turn off the burner, but there is something wrong with the stove and it refuses to respond. Now your choice is simple. Carefully, gradually, and with intention lift the lid, or have the pot blow up.

If your emotions keep building until the pot blows up —in other words, you hurt yourself or others—stop running and face your memories and feelings. Don't fight them. Instead, find someone to help you. Then learn how to release the emotions slowly and safely. You will come out at the other end stronger than before.

Sometime after the Vietnam war, a young couple, Carl and Angela, came to work with me at Angela's insistence. They were thinking of getting a divorce, but they had three children, and both members of the couple wanted the marriage to work. Shortly after the session began, Angela blurted out that she could not handle Carl's anger anymore. She felt he was becoming dangerous to her and the children. If he refused to deal with his memories of Vietnam, she couldn't stay with him.

When I glanced at Carl, I noticed that the words "Vietnam" and "anger" were large triggers for him. His face turned red. He tapped his foot. Suddenly he got up and raced out the door. Angela yelled after him, "You said you wouldn't run!" She began to cry. She and I talked for a while, then she made another appointment and left.

Angela did not keep her next appointment and I did not hear from either of them for several weeks. Then one afternoon Carl called. He and Angela had separated, but he very much missed his wife and kids. Instead of the anger retreating since their separation, his nightmares, memories, and rages had become worse. He was out of control and no longer able to keep a job or maintain relationships.

At our next session, I saw him alone. He decided to face himself and deal with his memories and feelings. It took incredible courage to do this, maybe as much courage as he had shown in Vietnam when he ran into enemy fire to save his friend.

When I asked Carl what he feared most, he said, "If I face my anger and grief, I will fall apart and be locked up in a mental ward for the rest of my life. I will scream and cry and never stop." Carl did not fall apart during our time together, although he did spend time crying. Instead he learned to talk about and deal with his anger in a safe way, and his doctor prescribed medications to help him through this difficult process. Yes, occasionally it happens that someone needs to be admitted to the hospital for what some people call a "nervous breakdown," especially after a severe trauma. But with the drugs and counseling now available, hospitalization rarely lasts long.

When you fear your emotions so much that you run or suppress them every time they are triggered, you stop growing, and the PTS symptoms worsen. You lose the intimate relationships you had with yourself, your mate, and your loved ones. If this is occurring in your life right now, it may be time to admit reality and accept your feelings.

These are some common emotions people experience when they suffer PTS: Ambivalence about life, loneliness, feelings of worthlessness, loss of purpose, depression, guilt and shame, feeling they did something wrong, humiliation over disabilities, frustration and desperation that progress is not occurring quickly enough, self destructive feelings, abandonment by the people around them especially when those people drop away over time, anger, resentment, and fear about things they don't understand or are not in their control, powerlessness.

Here are specific techniques to deal with some of your more difficult emotions: For many veterans with PTS or PTSD, there will come a time that the emotions will emerge when they encounter a trigger. Often this occurs after they get home and are safe and settled into a routine.

At times the emotion surfaces so quickly and powerfully, you feel as if you are re-experiencing your trauma. You feel as though you have lost all control of yourself, and the rage erupts at anyone that happens to be there at the time, usually your family, spouse, and children. Or you feel immense fear, guilt, and sadness, and you may shake, cry, and scream. Remember, emotions are okay. They are merely "energy in motion." It's what you do with them that counts.

When you feel strong emotions, you are not going crazy, but make sure you have someone with you to help you pace the rate of release so you remain safe. Usually the feelings will end in minutes, but may recur many times over the next weeks. Think of it like a well you have filled to overflowing and must empty back to a safe level. Eventually the emotions return to where they are manageable.

Many soldiers and veterans turn to alcohol and drugs to deal with the pain of their emotions. But don't forget, those emotions are still waiting there like a small bomb, ready to explode if you step on the trigger, regardless of when that occurs. And alcohol, because it is an addictive depressant, will make those feelings worsen over time.

CAUTION: FLOODING
In occasional situations, the emotions continue to surface for hours, sometimes days. If your emotions start to overwhelm you, please call your VA, counselor, or medical doctor immediately. Trained professionals can help you stem the tide with medications and counseling.

Because the most common emotion felt by veterans is anger, I will address it first.

ANGER:
When you examine your anger, you will usually find that it is rooted in fear. Most people, especially veterans, don't like to admit they feel fear, because fear makes them feel helpless and weak. Anger, on the other hand, makes them feel strong and in control. Anger is not a "bad" emotion, as many people believe. It's okay to be angry. Humans are all created with the same emotions, regardless of who they are or where they come from. We were given the emotion of anger for a good reason. It mobilizes and motivates people to act for justice and regain control of their destiny.

However, here is the problem with anger. Responding to threats with aggression, which is normal and often essential to survival in war, is no longer appropriate when you come home and reintegrate into society. When you get angry, you may want to lash out and hurt someone or yourself. Don't. What counts is how you act on your anger. It's **the action that becomes the problem, not the emotion.** If you face your anger and engage your logical forebrain, **you have a choice as to how to respond.**

The following are some suggestions to help you with your anger:

1. Think before you act.

2. **If you find yourself getting angry and having a hard time controlling yourself, leave immediately.** Make an agreement with family and close friends beforehand, while you are calm. Tell them that at this stage of your recovery you must leave, but you will return to address the problem with them later, when you have calmed down.

3. **Hit something that won't hurt you or someone else.** I had a client who would wear boxing gloves and hit boxes filled with sand. Another client filled a large cloth bag with rolled-up newspapers, hung it in the garage, and hit it with a baseball bat. Another bought old ceramic dishes at a thrift store, took them to the landfill, and smashed them. She needed the sound of the dishes crashing, as well as the physical activity, to let go of her anger.

Release your anger for short periods. Then stop and switch to something you enjoy. The new activity will help you return to the here and now. It is important to make a plan and determine what you would enjoy doing ahead of time, while you are thinking logically.

In a safe place where you are alone and won't frighten anyone, especially your children, smash something that's not important to anyone. Hit or kick a cardboard box, or set up a punching bag in the garage. Scream, yell, and cry. Tears often come after the screaming. Tears are normal, and are nature's way of releasing stress chemicals from your body.

A different approach might be to go out into the woods, away from everyone, and scream. Pretend the person you are mad at is sitting in front of you, and tell him or her exactly what you feel and how you want the person to be different. All these actions are means to release your emotions safely from your body so you don't hold them inside until you explode.

4. **Do hard physical activities.** These activities must exhaust you enough to release the tension in your muscles. For example, a major in the military began to train for marathons to release his pent-up energy. Here are a few more suggestions to trigger your thinking: sports such as football and soccer, workouts at the gym, running, working on a farm, yard work, construction, martial arts. I'm sure you and your friends can come up with many others. Studying a martial art (judo, karate, etc.) is particularly valuable because you will learn discipline and specific techniques to calm yourself and think before you act.

5. **After the body releases the emotion, you will feel more relaxed. At this point, write in your journal.** Ask yourself, "What am I so angry about?" Journal the answer. Then ask yourself, "What am I afraid of? What do I fear I have no

control over?" Journal about the fear that triggered the anger, and address the fear as well. Write an angry letter to the person you are mad at, then burn it. Or speak to a counselor or minister about it. Be honest.

Jeff, an Afghanistan war veteran, would get very angry at his wife and would hit her if she didn't do what he wanted her to do.

I asked him, "What does she do that makes you so angry?"

He said, "She won't follow orders."

"So what are you afraid will happen if she doesn't follow orders?"

"I'm angry, not scared," he retorted. "I never get scared."

"Just humor me," I said. " Imagine that you are someone else who does get scared. What might that person be afraid of?"

"I don't know. I guess he'd be scared that he didn't have control over what would happen in his life."

"And what might happen if this man had no control?"

He swallowed hard and said in a quiet voice, "She'd leave me and I'd be all alone. I've already lost all my buddies that I fought with. My friends don't think like I do anymore. My kids don't really want me around. I need her here with me, after all I've been through. I can't handle any more losses."

Jeff's fear underlying his anger dealt with loss—loss of the people in his life, and especially loss of control over others. He felt powerless and out of control over his life. Many veterans face the same issue. Loss of control over your life is indeed often the most frightening loss you will ever face. What are you afraid of losing? Your life or your loved one's life? Love? Closeness? Security? Money?

6. When you are feeling normal again, practice the deep breathing and relaxation exercises described in Step Four so that you can begin to use them the next time you feel angry. Meditation and prayer have also been found to greatly help reduce feelings of anger.

7. Notice your body when you feel angry. What physical changes take place? Where in your body do you hold your anger? Some people tend to stand straight with feet apart and head erect. They feel like forming a fist. Pay attention to what your body does when you are angry.

8. Take responsibility for your part in the problem. Work on changing your thinking and behavior. Ask yourself, "What do I gain from being angry?"

9. Take life one day at a time. Your anger may get more intense before it weakens. The cardinal rule is to make sure you don't physically or emotionally hurt yourself or others.

FEAR:
Fear is a useful, normal emotion that has kept humans alive over millennia. But if not overcome or dealt with, it can destroy us. In excess it becomes a paranoia, a constant anxiety, or a phobia, making life unmanageable. What you experienced in war is not normal. People don't deliberately place themselves in a situation where they or their friends are likely to die. Most veterans still believe they must always be strong and brave and that being afraid is not okay. But all people are afraid, and if they don't admit it, they are kidding

themselves. That underlying fear, even when you deny it and are not conscious of it, often prevents you from moving on and becoming the person you are capable of becoming. It holds you back from passion and purpose and keeps you from improving your life.

Here are some ways to deal with fear:

1. **Stop and identify when you are afraid.** How does fear feel in your body? Where are you feeling it? What are you thinking?

2. **Find a safe place where you can experience the fear.** Let yourself shake, cry, scream, laugh, or whatever lets you experience and move the energy of fear. If you have a dog, you may notice that his entire body shakes when he is afraid, and often he whimpers. After a few minutes, he has released the fear and the shaking stops. It's a normal and healthy way to discharge fear. So make sure you too release the stress from your body after a shock or fearful incident. If you don't, the emotion remains stuck in the body and you may develop tense muscles that can be physically very painful (e.g., back pain, headaches). Stress affects your immune system and decreases your resistance to disease.

Allow yourself to feel the emotions for about ten minutes. As with anger, it is important not to carry a loaded gun in case you mistake someone for an enemy and shoot her or him. If you need something to make you feel safe, carry pepper-spray, or carry a very heavy cane made specifically for defense. An FBI agent I met carries a cane everywhere he goes. In airports he pretends he has a limp and no one stops him.

3. Journal. Deal with your fear. Write down what you fear. How logical is your fear now that you are home? Rethink your fear. Is there really someone out there that wants to hurt you? What can you do to make you feel in more control of your life? (e.g., learn a martial art, solve a problem, etc.).

4. Don't act immediately on your fear. Look at it rationally. Sometimes what happens is that we become so afraid of the enemy and what it may do to us that we begin to lose touch with our principals and deeply held beliefs. We may even be willing to sacrifice freedom, love, justice, and democracy just to feel safe. Remember that our forefathers stood firm and refused to allow fear to overcome them. And that's why we have America now. So acknowledge your fear and feel it, but act out of love and reason. When you are afraid, always ask yourself before you act, "Am I acting out of fear?" Then consider how you really wish to act.

5. Ponder something you would like to do in your life but haven't done. Ask yourself, "Why don't I do it? What am I afraid of?" To get to the central issue, imagine yourself doing something you fear. Let's say you feel you have nothing in common with your partner anymore since you came back, and you want to ask her or him to make changes. You are afraid that your partner will be angry and throw you out of the house, or take the kids and everything you own. Or maybe you are afraid she or he will become very depressed and commit suicide.

Journal the following:

- Write down the situation.
- Ask yourself, "What am I afraid would happen if I asked her to make changes?"
- Keep asking, "And then what would happen?" until you have no more answers. Most of the time you will find that you are not nearly as afraid of the end result as you are of the process. Often you will realize that you can handle the process once you get to the end of your fears and see you have choices. Then ask yourself, "What am I afraid will happen if I *don't* ask her?" When you face your fears rather than avoid them, frequently you will be motivated to take charge and change your behavior. Your fear dissipates.
- When you have clearly looked at your fear, it is time to deal with the situation. Usually the anger and fear have lessened by then. In the previous example, you could talk to your partner about your fears and feelings. Tell them what they do and how you feel at the time. Take responsibility for your own feelings. No one *makes* you feel a certain way. You might say, "When you're so busy with the children and don't take time to do things with just me, that triggers my anger. I become afraid we have nothing in common anymore. I love you and I want to work on a solution together."

SADNESS AND GRIEF:
Sadness and grief occur when we lose something or someone, and also when we **think** we have lost something. A loss of belief, especially in a moral value we hold dear, can be as damaging as a physical loss.

Have you lost your mobility due to an injury? Has your brain been affected by an explosion? Have you lost your clear thinking? Your mate and children? Your friendships from the military? Your purpose in life? Your beliefs of invulnerability and that justice always prevails?

After a loss, or the fear of an imminent loss, most of us experience a period of denial. Our bodies and emotions become numb and our minds say, "This isn't happening." That's so we can handle the shock of the loss, or death and disaster, shortly after it occurs. But later the normal process of grieving continues.

Next, most people become angry. "Why did this have to happen to me? There is no justice. How could God let this happen?" But sometimes sadness and tears, not anger, come soon after a loss. All you want to do is cry and hide.

Many people begin to bargain with God. Let's say you were wounded and the doctor has told you he will have to remove your leg. You plead, "Please, God, if you just save my leg, I will go to church every week," or "I'll volunteer to help needy people." But since there is no way to save both the leg and your life, the doctor removes the leg.

Suddenly you realize what you have lost. You will never play baseball again or do many of the things you used to enjoy. You will never return to the construction job you had before you left. Hopelessness and depression set in. In most cases it may well take a year to resolve and accept your loss. Sometimes acceptance takes much longer. Don't get discouraged. This is the normal process of recovering from grief. You will need support from others as well as psychotherapy if the grief is too prolonged.

Here are some suggestions to help you deal with grief and loss:

1. **Allow your emotions to surface. Release them in a safe way.** Some people get stuck in depression because they stop the anger and sadness. When your tears flow, the energy in your body begins to flow as well. People often feel as though their tears are endless, or that it is weak to cry. That's what most of us have been taught in our culture. But tears are normal and need to be released. They will stop when you have emptied the well enough not to overflow. Tears have been designed by nature to release your stress chemicals. Most people say they feel more calm and at peace after crying.

2. **Journal about what happened and about your feelings.** Keep the energy flowing.

3. **Attend groups that deal with loss.** A VA group may be your best option at this point because other veterans will understand how you feel and will probably be most supportive.

4. **Change your thinking and behavior.** Change your thinking and soon your emotions will change (see Step Seven on changing your thinking). When emotions arise, ask yourself what you were thinking at the time. This is a conscious

urgent moment. Listen and acknowledge what you hear. They are powerful statements coming from within you. They are there to tell you something you need to know to heal, before you deny the emotions again. You will likely have to look at the trauma and break down your fear of the memory before you can start thinking about it differently.

GUILT AND SHAME:
Survivor guilt is beautifully expressed in this section of Patrick Overton's poem, "The Healing Wall":

Then I began to move my hands over the Wall –
over names I did not know, slow at first, and then faster, almost frantically –
at first not knowing why –
but then knowing –
I was looking for one name,
I was looking for the one groove my hands
would know the best,
the one that would confirm what I always knew
to be true but was afraid to admit
a name that wasn't there but should have been –
mine...the source of my guilt, my one great sin –
I had lived. I had come home.
I was no more deserving than any one of these names,
but I had survived.

Guilt and shame, frequently related, are common in veterans. Often the ambiguous rules of war create moral dilemmas and inner pain. You may feel you did something wrong while you were in the war and you feel guilt and shame about what you did. Or maybe you feel guilty that you left your spouse for such a long time and she had to take on all your duties at home. Or you feel you abandoned your children who needed you.

A Marine I counseled who had been in Vietnam felt enormous guilt for surviving when the rest of his platoon died. He had become separated from them, and when the Vietcong attacked, he had not been able to rescue them. Words I heard frequently from him were, "If only..." and "I should have..."

It's hard to move on when you carry a great deal of guilt and shame. Ask yourself, "Was I really in control of what happened?" If the answer is no, drop your guilt. You are not responsible. If the answer is yes, ask yourself? "Why did I do what I did? Was it because I didn't take the time to consider all the facts? Did I have the time? Did I do it out of fear? Or did I do it deliberately out of self-interest and anger?"

It is essential that you be honest and admit to yourself what really happened. Make amends if you can, then forgive yourself. If you did it out of fear, you will need to admit that you, like everyone else, are human. Fear can be an intense and overwhelming human emotion.

Here are some ways to deal with guilt and shame:

1. Journal about what happened.

2. Journal what your feelings and thoughts were at the time.

3. If you believe you did something wrong, admit it to yourself and to at least one other person whom you trust. Maybe that person will be your priest, rabbi, minister, or spiritual advisor.

4. Make amends to the people you wronged, if they are alive and if it is possible to contact them. If they are not alive, you are unable to contact them, or it would not be appropriate to contact them and tell them what happened, write them a letter and ask their forgiveness. Read it out loud. Then burn it. Burning is an important symbol for most people.

5. Ask for forgiveness in any way you need to and write yourself a forgiveness letter.

Glenn, one of the veterans I counseled, had struggled for several years to forgive himself for killing innocent women and children during the Vietnam War. He could not come to peace with what he had done. I knew he attended the Catholic church regularly and I also knew his priest. When I asked Glenn whether it would be okay for me to contact Father Tom, he hesitated, then said, "Yes." Father Tom called Glenn the next day, and they met a couple of hours later. After Father Tom talked to Glenn and granted him absolution, Glenn finally let go of his guilt.

STEP TEN:
Reconnect spiritually.

In this section I am not referring to any specific religious or spiritual beliefs. I speak of "spirit" as a power greater than ourselves that we have learned to believe in, connect to, and trust over our years of life.

The trauma of war is considered by many to be a moral issue and a "soul trauma" as well as a physical, emotional, and mental one. Although some veterans have not lost their belief in a loving spiritual being because of the war, many others question their faith. Why would a loving God allow the hatred, destruction, suffering, and death of war and not intervene? Why has God deserted us? Why did the creator of everything not make the world and humanity better than this? Does God not care about us? Does God even exist?

War often delivers a deep soul wound to veterans' identities, senses of morality, and relationships to society. They may feel abandoned, depressed, and angry at God. They have lost their sense of purpose and their reason for being on Earth. Many of these feelings come from the emptiness of not being spiritually connected, of having lost trust and faith in a higher power.

Twenty Steps to Help You Heal

In an article in *Clinical Psychological Review* (December 2009), VA psychologist Bret Litz and his colleagues wrote that the greatest lasting harm to veterans comes from moral injury and guilt, especially survivor guilt. He or she may wonder, "Why was I one of the people who came back, when others didn't?" Many also have the guilt of killing or hurting others. Regardless of which religion you may have been raised in, most shun taking human life unless absolutely necessary. The messages you received in your house of worship and your society are often directly in opposition to what you have been required to do in war, creating a tremendous internal moral struggle. One of the veterans I spoke to recently kept repeating the question, "How do I reconcile what I learned in my church and at home with what my culture and government needed me to do? War is hell. Did I make the right decisions, or should I have done things differently? It hurts me inside all the time."

Not only are soldiers faced with making tough decisions about when to defend themselves, but also how to do it, and to what degree. These dilemmas can lead military personnel to question their decisions and actions after the fact. A soldier's duty is to follow orders, but what if those orders are contrary to his or her personal and spiritual beliefs?

If you were left with physical and emotional combat injuries you may have to create a new identity and a new lifestyle. To complicate this identity struggle further, the ambiguous rules of war can create moral dilemmas for you and other military personnel. You may be left with powerful perceptions that the deployment was a failure or was, from the onset, immoral and unjustified. But remember, you did what you believed needed to be done at that time to protect your country and loved ones. Perhaps later you felt it wasn't right. Perhaps it was not a just war after all, but it was what you had to do.

In his book *War and The Soul*, Ed Tick writes that sometimes it is essential, after the war, to take veteran warriors back to the actual battlefield and help them, as a group, rework their memories and forgive themselves. Several groups of Vietnam veterans have done just that, and the process has worked miracles for them.

Tick has also begun programs in the South where present-day warriors are welcomed home and taken care of as were warriors of old. Many Native American villagers used to gather around in a circle and welcome the warriors home from the battlefield. They were reincorporated into the community in a healing ceremony where they were held and nurtured. Everyone would listen and give witness to the warriors' stories, and also mourn with them. The whole community would share in the guilt and sorrow of what had happened, and then take care of their warriors until they were healed.

Tick has found this approach very helpful for our returning veterans. He is gathering circles of people to welcome veterans home, let them express their feelings and what happened to them. The circle shares the responsibilities of the war and helps the veterans in any way they need help.

It is essential for us as a culture to *own* our wars and to collectively take the responsibility and guilt for the atrocities that have happened during them. We have asked you, our military people, to go to war to protect us, and we need to face the realities of war squarely instead of divorcing ourselves from them. Then we need to all join together and take care of you.

For family members and friends of veterans, Tick has also written a book called *When Someone You Love Suffers from Post Traumatic Stress*, published in 2011. I suggest that you check out this book, as well as *War and the Soul*.

As family members it is not our place to determine as right or wrong what you, our loved ones, have done. I remember a time when I was young, listening to the news with my father. I became furious at the actions of some of the soldiers. He looked at me sadly and said, "Oh, Anna, you have no idea what you would do in that situation."

As one Vietnam veteran wrote to me, "We did what we had to do. We can't ignore it, eject it out of our lives, or exorcise it out of our souls. We have to learn to live with it, because it will always be part of us. But we should not have it control how we live our lives now. . . . My Native American friend taught me that I was a warrior. Not because I fought in a war, but because I was willing to do what I believed needed to be done to protect those I loved, my neighbors, and my country."

If you want to connect or reconnect with and trust a higher power again, how do you do it? Here are some suggestions:

1. Meditation and prayer.
I won't give you a definition of prayer or meditation. You need to define these words for yourself. Some people see meditation and prayer as two sides of a coin, defining meditation as a way to empty their minds of all thoughts and allow their higher power to speak to them, and prayer as a way for them to speak to their higher power.

Recently neurologists have discovered a small area in the brain that is activated when a person meditates or prays, allowing him or her to experience spirituality and a connection to God. The amygdala calms down, and the pathways in a certain area in the brain open up and connect with something higher than the ordinary self. Meditation and prayer also open people up to love and compassion for themselves and everyone around them.

I suggest that the most powerful way to meditate and pray is in a group, especially in a circle that connects you with people who care about one another, who can understand what you are going through, and who show compassion to one another. For many of you, prayer may remind you that the ultimate goal of war is to end war. General (later President) Dwight D. Eisenhower once said that war should be a last resort, used only as a means to end wars and to bring peace, democracy, and safety to the world.

2. Let go. Use the first three steps of a twelve-step program to help you let go of needing to be in control of everything that happens to you. Although at present, to my knowledge, there are no twelve-step programs specifically for veterans and their families, several people have suggested that one be started. Some have even mentioned a few word changes in the twelve steps to better serve veterans. The following is a possible version of the first three steps, as mentioned on the Internet.

- We admitted we were powerless over the effects of war, on ourselves and our families and that our lives had become unmanageable.
- Came to believe that a power greater than ourselves could restore us to sanity.
- Made a decision to turn our will and our lives over to the care of our higher power as we understand that higher power.

3. Write down in your journal what you have believed in the past, and what you believe now. Who are you? What are your moral and ethical beliefs and core values? What is your worldview? What do you think mankind's purpose is here on earth? What is the meaning of life? What is your purpose in being here? War requires you to do many things that bring out your "dark side" and are not in adherence to most people's cultural and religious beliefs and norms. How do you reconcile what you had to do with these beliefs?

4. Visit a church, temple, or mosque, or join a spiritual discussion group. Talk to a spiritual advisor of your choice who will listen to you and empathize as well as give you advice.

5. Read spiritual literature that is uplifting and inspirational. Judgmental books are not for you at this point. Look on the Internet and in church libraries, public libraries, and bookstores. Ask friends and other veterans for recommendations of books they have found valuable.

6. Create a ritual. Do yoga, meditate, and/or pray at least three times a day, even for short periods, such as a few minutes. Yoga helps you relax and tone your body but it also encourages you to focus your mind and become more aware of the internal flow of your energy. It can aid in balancing and connecting the mind, body, and spirit and can open you up to meditation.

Meditate on your breathing and look at a blank white wall until all your thoughts fade into the distance and your mind is blank. This state is very restful to the mind. Sometimes you receive great insights if you ask for help.

You can also think of a "mountaintop" experience you have had and meditate on it. Some people have had special dreams or visions, out-of-body experiences, or even near-death experiences. If you've ever had such experiences, treasure them and hang on to the feeling they gave you.

7. Several times a day, speak to a personal God who is listening to you and cares about you. Create an image of God in your mind. What does your God look like? A cloud? A light? A man? A woman? Tell God your problems. Start by trusting God just a little, if that's all you can do. One of my clients quoted Matthew 17:20, the verse in the Bible that says that if you have faith as small as a mustard seed you will be able to move mountains. He said, "A mustard seed. That's pretty small. I think I can do that."

8. Resolve your shame and guilt. If you feel at fault for something that happened and think that you "are not good enough," or you did something wrong, ask yourself, "Was I in control of the situation?" If not, let the guilt go. It's not yours to carry.

When you feel shame, you think you let yourself and others down, and all you want to do is withdraw. Don't. Face your shame and guilt. If you were in control of what happened and you **chose** to do something that hurt others, be honest about your mistakes and take responsibility for them. Take an honest moral inventory of what you have done in the past and own your mistakes. Share the inventory with someone who will understand. Shame dissipates when you feel understood and you receive empathy. Then ask for forgiveness and make amends.

But apologizing and asking for forgiveness is of little value if you don't change your behavior. I imagine most of you heard about former U. S. Representative Anthony Weiner who, after being caught in a public scandal, followed all the steps above, but did not change his behavior. Instead he kept doing what he had always done, so his apologies meant little.

Also know that sometimes shame and guilt are positive emotions. When you feel them, you know that you have a conscience. This is good. In the bigger view of life, our consciences shape social behavior and help our communities and species survive.

9. Forgive yourself and others. Here is another issue all of us must face. Inside each of us there is what we call a "light side" and a "dark side." One of the clients I met with was the wife of a Vietnam veteran. She said that her husband could not forgive himself for allowing that dark side to come out while at war. He could not forgive himself for killing and torturing people, for burning villages, and for walking away from screaming children and women. He spent a lot of time muttering in his sleep and talking to God. But he could not believe that God could forgive him for what he had done. He could not *accept* the forgiveness of God. Forty years later, he is still sure he will spend eternity in hell. In plain words you must *accept* the forgiveness of God and of yourself before you can let the guilt go.

How can you forgive yourself?

- **Accept that you are human and have limitations.** As I've said, humans have both light and dark sides. Instead of becoming defensive and isolated, admit that you have a dark side. The truth is that war is dark, and when you live with continual violence and are fighting for your life, the dark side comes out. Anger, hatred, violence, and even torture are the results. If you wish the dark side to stop coming out at the most inopportune times now that you are home, you will need to forgive and learn to love even that side of yourself.
- **Confess to another person what you did,** someone you trust who won't judge you, like a fellow veteran, minister, priest, or rabbi. Acknowledge what you believe you did wrong, first to yourself, then to a spiritual advisor, and ask for forgiveness.
- **Allow others to love you, hug you, and forgive you.** Allow yourself to accept the forgiveness of your higher power and of others. Open your heart and let in the light—the feelings of forgiveness.

- **Cultivate your "light side."** Show compassion and love for others and yourself, and allow your actions now and in the future to come out of love instead of fear. Do random acts of kindness daily. Before you act, give yourself permission to think for a moment and make a conscious choice about how you will act. What do you wish your motivation to be? Fear? Anger? Love? Showing kindness can be as simple as helping someone cross the street or smiling at him or her.
- **Ask your higher power to forgive you.** Most religions believe that their higher power is always open to forgiving followers who are sincere. Envision your higher power standing in front of you. Dialogue with that benevolent wise being. Ask him/her/it for forgiveness and imagine that entity forgiving you. Then allow forgiveness into your heart. Feel the burden you have been carrying lift.
- **Now it is time to forgive yourself.** Visualize your dark side standing near you and talk to it. Repeat "I forgive myself" out loud or in your mind, many times a day.
- **Write yourself a forgiveness letter and read it out loud every day, especially just before you go to bed.**
- **Take time to ask yourself the following questions:** What have you gained from adversity? What would you do differently next time? What did you learn?

10. **Create an altar or a sacred space.** Discover what helps you feel more spiritual and closer to your higher power. If you

have come from a church or religion that uses some kind of incense, your sense of smell may be your connection. Music or chanting is another way to connect. Practice reassuring rituals. One of the veterans I spoke to recently returned to his native culture to attend rituals and to do a vision quest. He said it helped him regain his purpose and reason for living. He is now much less depressed and is moving in a new direction.

You might use paintings, pictures, statuary, or anything else tangible that is important to you. Flowers and plants are alive and will move you to feeling alive. Place them somewhere you consider to be a special place in your house. The altar will help reconnect you to your higher self whenever you need it.

Create some form of art (see Step Fourteen) and place it on the altar. Art often expresses a spiritual component of ourselves. It seems to me that any artistic expression, when motivated by a spiritual compassion, will bring out your soul, will live in your creation, and will touch others.

STEP ELEVEN:
Deal with memories.

A word of warning for people with severe PTS: memories often set off emotions that trigger a reliving of the trauma. If you are at home and need to deal with your memories, call someone you trust who can help you in case you need her or him. Ask the person to stay with you, if possible, until the memories have passed.

If you, like many veterans, feel compelled to repeat your story over and over again in an attempt to master the event, don't let people tell you that there is something wrong with you. This "need to tell" your memories and have someone witness what happened to you is common and normal, and can be very helpful. As a matter of fact, telling your story is one of two kinds of therapy found to be most effective in healing PTSD. Talking helps your mind release the memory of the trauma and rebuild it or change it. Just make sure you are safe when memories come to you.

Until recently, scientists have not fully understood what happens in your brain when you retell your trauma, except that the emotional energy charge in the amygdala is decreased. But new research has revealed that memory is much more complex than previously believed.

It was once thought memory did not change. While it was obvious that people had different perceptions of an event, it was believed that once that memory was seared into the brain, it did not change, even after many retellings.

Then in 1999 Dr. Karim Nader discovered that memory was not nearly as stable as people thought. He and others showed that reactivating a memory by remembering or retelling it actually destabilized it, placing it into a flexible state where it could be permanently altered.

Each time you remember or retell your memories, they change. Amazing! It is now obvious why remembering and retelling can be so powerful, both for the negative and the positive. The following suggestions are meant to give you ways of dealing with your emotions, but also ways to remember, retell, and rebuild your trauma in a more positive and less traumatizing way.

If possible, read Part One, then work through Step One on stabilization and Step Seven on changing your thinking before you continue with Step Eleven. Journaling can bring up powerful memories. You need to recognize common symptoms of PTS and how you can handle them when you feel unstable. Practice your breathing and relaxation techniques (Step Four) to calm you while you journal or remember.

Here are a few suggestions on how to deal with your memories:

1. **Write in a journal.** Many people have told me that journaling their memories and feelings has been the most effective

therapy for them. Writing helps release the feelings and memories from the brain instead of allowing them to continue swirling and enlarging there. It is best to journal daily, as well as whenever the trauma comes to mind or you feel a strong emotion. Some people carry their journals with them wherever they go, even to work or school.

- Begin by journaling your feelings as often as you can. You can journal about all your emotions, even positive ones, such as happiness, joy, and contentment.
- Here is an example: Write, "I am feeling so angry right now. . . ." and continue to tell what you are angry about and what happened to trigger this anger. Maybe you will refer back to the war, and maybe you won't. That's not important. What is important is getting your feelings down on paper.
- If the emotion takes over, express it in a safe way (see Step Nine). After you have expressed your feelings, you may want to diffuse them by checking what other emotions lay underneath the obvious ones. For example, when you look closely at anger, you may find that you are afraid of something. Ask yourself, "What am I afraid of?" It may be fear of having no control over the situation. Loss of control is very frightening and is one of the main causes of PTS. If your partner says or does something you don't like and you get angry and blow up, ask yourself why. The situation might upset you because you can't control what is happening and what the consequences of that action will be. Maybe underneath you're afraid that he or she will leave you.

- List what you can do to improve your situation. In our example, rather than yell at your partner, you could sit down quietly and tell him or her what you are feeling. Then ask for his or her point of view, and work together to find a solution to your problem. If that doesn't work, see whether the two of you can seek counseling together. (More techniques for problem solving and decision making are discussed in Step Three.)
- Look at your part in the problem, write it down in your journal, and decide what you want to change. Remember, you can't change other people's behaviors, but you can change your own. When one person changes, usually the other person's response will change as well. Patterns of behavior develop over time as they are repeated. You may have observed and learned these patterns in your family while you were growing up. Do you usually respond in anger to certain problems, blow up, and then blame your partner for what happened? Experiment with handling the problem differently. Set your anger aside with your rational mind, listen to your partner. and then accept your part in the pattern. If you are still angry, you can leave and run or do rigorous exercises to release it from your body.
- What lesson, if any, can you learn from what happened? Journal about it. Recognizing the lessons you can learn by going through hard times is difficult at first, but becomes easier as you go along. Maybe you learned you really do have more control over yourself

than you thought. Maybe you learned that thinking before you act on your feelings helps you get what you want, now that you are home and not in a war zone.
- If you are able, place yourself in the shoes of the other person. Ask yourself how he or she might be feeling and why. Often he or she is also afraid of something. Again, write it down.

Several years ago my daughter studied ballet with a prima ballerina from Hungary. After each class, my daughter came home angry. Mrs. Grunethal (not her real name) had yelled at the girls again. "You all look like cows! Won't you ever learn?" Now, keep in mind that the girls she was teaching were all exceptional dancers, most heading toward careers in dance. My daughter and her friends, afraid of losing their positions in the company, refused to speak up. I told my daughter that her instructor's behavior probably had little to do with what the girls were doing, but my daughter had difficulty believing she was not an inferior dancer in some way.

One day I sat down with her and we came up with a plan of how to handle the situation. We spent time finding out about Mrs. Grunethal's life in Hungary under Communist rule and her escape to America. Suddenly the yelling and need for control made sense to my daughter. Although she could not change the situation, she had changed her perspective. Instead of anger, she felt empathy and sadness toward her instructor. Her relationship with Mrs. Grunethal changed almost immediately.

When I asked my daughter what she had learned, she said, "Two things: I'll never treat my students that way, and

I will look underneath to see what's going on with the other person whom I'm having problems with." She and another woman now own a dance company, and she lives what she learned.

2. Retell your trauma story. This technique is one that therapists have learned can be very effective in trauma recovery, when the person is ready. It may take time before you feel ready to tell your story. There is no need to rush. The goal is to reduce and manage your anxiety and fears. Retelling your story many times over usually lessens your reaction to your trauma and defuses the intensity of the memory. It breaks certain networks and connections in the brain.

After a while, you will be able to face the trauma without a severe bodily and emotional reaction. Telling your story usually helps you direct your anger at the right target (e.g., your combat experience), not at your loved ones. Furthermore, the anger will diffuse over time.

I remember when my father needed to share his memories of war. They would begin to tumble out of his mouth whenever he remembered. At the time, most people around him, including my mother, were terrified of negative emotions, especially anger, and they silenced him. He stopped speaking of his memories entirely, but that did not stop his outbursts of anger. Only now the outbursts were directed at the family, instead of at what he had witnessed in the war.

If your memories trigger your emotions to such an extent that you are having difficulty functioning, you must see a therapist who can guide you through this process. Always start by telling yourself that **the incident that triggered the**

trauma is in the past. You survived and you are safe now. You don't need to be afraid of your memories. They are just that: memories. Record your stories on a digital recorder as you tell them. Replay them later, or just keep them. Your story will evolve over time.

- Tell your story to a therapist, a trusted friend, or even an animal. Although repeating your story over and over again may not always be necessary to recovery, people have found that each time they recount the trauma to someone they trust, the impact of the trauma lessens. When you talk to a trusted friend, tell the person that you don't need advice. You just need him or her to listen. The energy from the emotion dissipates further each time you tell your memory. Sharing your story also helps you make sense of what happened and reveals what you can learn from the experience.
- If there is no one around to whom you can tell your story, journal it. Many of my clients say that journaling was the most important step in their recovery.
- Attend group therapy, such as a **VA group**, church group, twelve-step program, or online group on the Internet. As humans we need to have someone witness our feelings and to feel accepted, regardless of what we have done or what has happened to us. At the same time, avoid telling your stories to people who may judge you or join you in your depression, fears, or anger. Remember the veteran I mentioned earlier who talked only to his veteran friends? United

in their depression, eventually they got drunk and played Russian Roulette, with tragic consequences. Select a group with a positive leader and other individuals who will encourage you as well as commiserate with you. In a healthy group, you should feel supported and have a better outlook on life by the time you leave.

After the Vietnam war, Bob, a Marine living near Spokane, finally went to therapy when his flashbacks became so intense and frequent that he was no longer able to function. He enrolled in a research program conducted by Dr. Miles McFall at the VA, which included group support. The group told and retold their stories until the emotions finally decreased in intensity. At first Bob complained that Dr. McFall was not a veteran. He said he didn't understand why we "psychologist types" were trying to help veterans when we really didn't understand any of them. However he did admit that the group literally saved his life. When I told him that, no, I didn't understand exactly what he had been through, and that it was essential that he spend time in veterans groups who did, he harrumphed. I went on to explain that psychologists did, however, know how to help people with PTSD because they had worked with so many and had observed which techniques had worked for them, like group therapy and retelling their memories.

3. Maintain prolonged contact with the environment and/or situation that triggers you. With a technique called Prolonged Environment Therapy (PET), used effectively for many years to help people overcome phobias, a person confronts her or his fears in a safe environment, either in the imagination or in the real world. The goal is to decrease your fears and to reinforce that you, not your memories, are in control of your life. The process must be done step-by-step if it is going to help you learn to overcome your fear of a place or situation. PET works best if you begin with a lesser fear and gradually work up to the major trauma.

In "the good old days," we used to tell people to "buck up," and to jump back on the proverbial horse after falling off. For example, if as a child you couldn't swim and you almost drowned, a parent might have thrown you back into the ocean to make you face your fears immediately. Well, sometimes the results of this "tough love" were positive, but often they were catastrophic. For many, the practice etched the fear more deeply into the brain, turning it into a phobia almost impossible to extinguish.

If fear is limiting your life and you want to recover, you cannot ignore it. I have dealt with several veterans who were unable to leave their homes, to walk into a crowded place, or to sit near a door or window for fear of attack. They felt exposed and vulnerable. Some moved into the mountains or the forest to get away from people altogether.

If you choose to use this immersion technique, here are some suggestions:

a. Imagine the environment you fear. Many returning veterans who are severely stressed find they are afraid, or at least very uncomfortable with, specific places. These can be closed spaces like elevators and unfamiliar buildings, or open ones like roads, and streets. Or they may experience other fears, such as social phobias: leaving the house, being in crowds, being cornered, sitting near doors and windows, and hearing loud noises like gunshots (which may only be a car backfiring or a fireworks display). Although you may not always consciously remember why, any of these places and events can trigger you back to your war experiences.

Here is an example of how to help extinguish the fear by using your imagination:

Let's say you are afraid of being in a room with many people, and therefore have given up attending social events, but this is a behavior you'd like to change.

- Imagine standing outside a crowded room or party, looking in from a distance, far enough away to feel safe. Remind yourself that you are home now, not in the war, and that you are safe.
- Repeat this exercise over several days. Each time, imagine and journal about moving closer and closer to the party until you actually walk inside. Each day, write down what you are feeling in your body as you approach. Does your heart pound? Are you perspiring? Are your legs shaking?
- When you can imagine being in the party without wanting to scream and leave, then imagine yourself talking to people and enjoying the event. Reaching this level of comfort may take several days or even weeks. Don't get discouraged. You are moving forward.

- When you are ready, actually attend a function with just a few people. The next time, add more people. If you need to leave, don't be discouraged. Simply continue the imagining and journaling until the fear gradually dissipates. Your fears will shrink as your mind realizes that a crowded room no longer represents danger, now that you are home.
- When you feel you've conquered one fear, then choose a more pressing fear to work on and repeat the same sequence of steps.

An emerging technology called virtual reality may help you, the veteran, to process your feelings by imagining the environment you were in when the trauma occurred. Virtual reality equipment is being installed in many VA therapy rooms. Of course, it is best to use these programs in conjunction with psychotherapy. Read Step Nineteen to learn more about this and other groundbreaking new technologies.

b. Maintain prolonged contact with actual triggering environments: This is called the "real-world practice" approach, based on the idea that the easiest way to lose your fear is to actually experience the environment you fear. But unlike the thrown-in-the-ocean example cited above, the fear-producing environment should be experienced gradually, a little at a time, so as not to overwhelm you and worsen your fears.

Slowly reintroduce yourself to traumatic environments, as you did in your imagination in the previous exercise. Journal your reactions. Use deep breathing and relaxation exercises when you need to. Often this technique is better done with another person you trust rather than alone, in case your memories flood you with emotions.

Ray, a veteran of Afghanistan, returned with PTSD. At first he couldn't walk into a public building such as a restaurant without experiencing a panic attack. After working with a Vietnam veteran from the Veterans Center Mobile Unit for several months, using both imagining and real-world practice, he was able to meet me in a Mexican restaurant for lunch. He admitted he still could not bring himself to sit near the door or next to a window, but he was very proud of himself for not becoming so anxious that he had to leave. In fact, he tolerated being in the restaurant for over an hour.

Alex, an Iraq veteran, was unable to leave his house without having panic attacks. Today he is able to take a bus to work. He credited prolonged exposure to his feared environment as the most effective technique for his recovery.

4. Release your trauma memories symbolically. Our minds constantly work with symbols. For each person, these symbols may be different. A dog means love to me, and I feel warm and happy inside when I see one. But to someone else who was bitten as a child, a dog may be frightening. A snake reminds me of the garter snakes I grew up with on our ranch in central Canada. I think they are slithery, but certainly not frightening. To someone else, snakes might be terrifying.

Different religions and cultures use symbols as well. In a Christian church, the cross symbolizes Christ's crucifixion. In Western culture, a wedding band symbolizes a person's commitment to her or his partner. Your military uniform is a symbol of your commitment to your country and your willingness to give the ultimate sacrifice.

Rituals and ceremonies can be used to mark a life change or transition, allowing a person to let go of the old and move into the new. Native Americans use many such ceremonies. In the Jewish faith, a bar mitzvah symbolizes the passage of a boy into manhood.

Some people, when they are ready to move on, toss their outmoded or outgrown symbols into a stream or river and watch them float away. They don't need them anymore. Others use burning as a way to release and let go. In some cases, such as when you decide to let go of an angry letter you have written to someone, you are glad to burn that symbol. But many times the ceremony may let go of a symbol and a time that you once cherished or are still grieving (e.g., a death or relationship), but you know that it's time to move on.

You are home now. It is time to leave your military life behind and move forward in your civilian life, time to let go of the war memories and create new ones. But you are the only one who knows what your personal symbols of the war are, and what they mean to you, and when you are ready to release them.

Here are a few suggestions to help you let go:

- Respectfully take off your dog tags and lay them in a safe place. Pack away your uniform. It's not that you aren't proud of your military service, but the act signals that you are now ready to move on into civilian life. Buy some new clothes that indicate who you are now.

- Write down, then burn your stories of your war experiences, fears, pain, resentments, and anger. Or throw the papers into the river and watch them float away.
- Pack your unloaded gun and place it somewhere safe.
- Create a new symbol—one that reminds you that you have survived and are growing in strength and compassion. For you, a veteran, that may be a photo of yourself in street clothes, posed with family and loved ones or a favorite pet, or at a job you enjoy. As you look at the photo frequently, your mind will gradually incorporate this new image of yourself.
- Celebrate your new life. The celebration can include anything from hosting a gathering of friends to going off alone to the forest to listen to the wind in the trees or to a brook flowing through a meadow.

5. Change your memories of the trauma.
What do you choose to focus on in your memory? You have a choice. Your memories depend very much on your perception of the event that occurred, which might differ from someone else's perception. Do you ever compare your childhood memories with those of a parent, brother, sister, or friend? Your memories will likely differ from theirs, even though each of you experienced the same event, because everyone focused on different aspects of that event. Each of us remembers our own stories in the context of what was happening to us at the time.

Interestingly, when you incorporate new facts about the event, your memories will change as well. For example, maybe you are angry at your father for something he did when you were a child. If you find out that your father was very ill that day, you won't think of him in the same way as you did in the past. Your feelings of compassion will make you less judgmental of him. In the case of combat memories, imagine that you talk to another veteran who was in your unit, and he tells you that your commander, whom you saw as cruel, was beaten severely as a child and abandoned. Would having that additional knowledge change your feelings about him?

Scientists such as Dr. Joseph LeDoux from New York University and his research team have recently discovered that as you replay your memories, you reawaken and recombine them as many times as you remember that particular event. Unknowingly (or sometimes knowingly), you add new details and tweak the facts. Each time you remember the event, you replace that version with a slightly different one, until eventually all you can recall is your story of your story of the original memory.

Because memories change each time you remember them, you are able to make them more or less traumatic, depending on how you choose to see them. Rebuilding your memories using different data or perceptions about the event will eventually change your feelings. Now you have a choice as to how and what you want to remember about your trauma.

The most important question you need to ask yourself is, "Where is my focus when I remember my trauma?" Do you focus on all the terrible events that happened? That's the case for most people. But what if you chose to remember some good things as well? What if you also remembered someone coming to rescue you, or someone supporting you during the tragedy? Were you aware of anyone trying to help you? Where did the bullet hit you—could things have been worse? Remind yourself that you survived. Picture your mate or friends praying for you, and the bullets missing you or at least failing to kill you.

Several techniques work to change or reconsolidate a memory of a trauma, and thereby alter the emotions associated with it. One is called rebuilding your memories.

Here are two ways to begin using this technique:

- **Do some research about your traumatic event and incorporate any new facts** you learn that you didn't know back then. Check with other people who were present or involved in the event. What might they have seen or understood that you didn't? Are there any new facts that you can include in your memory and choose to focus on the next time you remember?

    Clarence, who was seriously injured during an Al Qaeda attack, felt he had been left to die in a deserted building. He lay there for what seemed a very long time and eventually drifted into unconsciousness. Several hours later, he woke up and realized he had been airlifted to a medical facility. Though his physical injuries were severe, the most painful part of his memory of the attack was the belief that his unit had not tried to rescue him. He felt abandoned by his "brothers" who should have been there for him. Clarence never returned to the battlefield, and the memory haunted him for years.

Recently Clarence wrote to some of the men from his unit and got their take on the story. Their perceptions were very different from his. They told him that they had tried several times to rescue him, but had been unable to get near the building until nightfall. They felt immense guilt and shame at letting him down.

The veterans from this unit now meet annually to share their stories, cry and laugh together, and support each other. All the men have begged Clarence for forgiveness for not being there for him when he needed them. Clarence now remembers the story of his trauma very differently from how he once did.

- **Remember your trauma as you originally experienced it.** Journal it, or describe it to someone else. **Then, at least ten minutes but no longer than two hours later** (the period when the brain rebuilds the memory, according to Dr. LeDoux's research team), **remember the trauma again, incorporating the new facts** that you've learned about it. Write the new version down and reread it several times. From now on, when you remember the new memory and tell it to someone else, always include the updated facts.

STEP TWELVE:
Take responsibility for yourself.

WHEN VETERANS COME HOME FROM their tour of duty and need to reintegrate into society, they often feel disenfranchised, useless, and lost. They begin to think that they no longer belong in their families and their country, and that they have no purpose or control over their lives.

In some ways living at home is more difficult than living in the military. In the latter you had a specific structure, a defined job and purpose, and a commanding officer to help you make decisions. Now you are on your own in a loosely ordered world that does not necessarily conform to your values and beliefs. People look at life differently and act differently than you are used to. No wonder you feel lost.

But you have a strength most other people at home do not have. You have learned to work as a team and take responsibility for yourself and others. In time you will find new purpose at home. Remember, feelings and thoughts will come and go, and you can work on changing them. As we discussed earlier, you can choose where you focus your thoughts. Ask yourself, "Does focusing on all the negative things happening in my life and the world help anyone, including myself? Does it make me happy? Does it attract the kind of people I want in my life? Does it allow me to reintegrate at home?"

You have choices about your actions, probably more than you've ever had before. You do not need to act on your feelings or say out loud the things you are thinking. You can choose whether to apply for a job, whether to come to work on time, how to act when under stress, how to respond in a relationship. Think of yourself as your own commander. If you admired someone in the military and wanted to be like him or her, ask yourself what decisions that person might make.

I saw a recent TV show on veterans who come home from combat only to join violent motorcycle gangs that fight, rob, and kill. Something in these veterans wouldn't let them stop fighting, couldn't stop their need for excitement and the flow of adrenaline they had become accustomed to during the war. Although I understand their predicament, I also know these veterans had choices. They could have dealt with their addictions to adrenaline, and possibly drugs, in ways other recovering addicts do. They could have chosen to become involved in activities that were exciting but positive. Instead they *chose* to delve into their dark side.

You too have a choice to make about your life, now that you are home. Life away from battle is not trivial. You can make a difference in our country.

After the end of the first Iraq war, I met with a young veteran who had chosen a negative way of life in order to recreate the excitement he had felt on the battlefield. But his choices had created many problems for him. He'd lost his family, his job, and eventually he spent several weeks in jail. When we looked at all the legal activities he could substitute for what he was doing that would still be exciting, he remembered how much he had enjoyed ski-jumping prior to his enlistment in the army. He realized that ski-jumping was more fun, and just as exhilarating, as racing cars and crashing them on the freeway. In time he went on to join a rescue team at the local ski resort.

It takes a conscious effort to take responsibility for yourself. You can live responsibly only when you are honest with yourself and look clearly at your feelings, your thoughts, and your actions. Consider how you react during an argument with a family member or friend. Do you run out, get in your car, and screech away at fifty miles per hour? Do you punch the person? Or do you stop, take a minute to think, then consciously choose to go for a walk or write in your journal to blow off steam? Do you rationally assess what is going on inside and what you need to do next? Are you willing to look at yourself instead of automatically blaming other people and circumstances for the situation?

Examine your part in the argument, not just the other person's part. Blaming others won't help *you* solve your problems. As I mentioned earlier, you can't make people change. You can only change yourself. Ask yourself, "What was I doing before the argument occurred? How did I react? Is there something the other person did or said that triggered me emotionally? What may have happened in my past that is similar to what is happening now? Did that memory trigger my anger? Can I deal with my feelings, or do I need to cool off, then come back, sit down with the person, and talk with him or her in a caring and understanding way when I am ready? If there is something I do (like shaking my finger at people) that causes others to react negatively, will I choose to continue that behavior?" How you act and react, what you decide to do, what you say to yourself and others, is up to you. No one else can make those choices for you.

On the other hand, take responsibility only for *your own* actions, not for other people's choices. Sometimes you can influence them for the negative or positive, but ultimately they must be responsible for their own choices, just as you are. You are not in control of others. You are in control only of the things you say to them, the information you give them, and how you act and react. That is your responsibility.

If someone is cruel or uncaring toward you, you have a choice whether to react or to walk away. What is it about the person's actions that triggers your reaction? Might it be something you don't like in yourself?

A couple I met with were headed for a divorce. Gavin frequently blew up at Jan for not being a responsible person. He said she had lost her job again and he couldn't pay all their bills. He did, however, acknowledge that she was a wonderful mother to their two young children.

Jan admitted she had lost several jobs because she had come to work late or stayed home when the children were ill or she felt they needed her. However, she did not agree with Gavin that her actions were irresponsible. As a mother, she believed the needs of her children were more important than her job.

Gavin said that, as a child, his parents had taught him to always be truthful and take responsibility for his actions. If he failed to do a good job, he was severely punished. He hated himself for disappointing his parents, whom he said he loved very much. He had tried hard all his life to be responsible. Now, when he perceived his wife as being irresponsible at work, it triggered him to the point of rage. By the end of the session, both understood how the other person felt, and they were able to reach a compromise. What helped them solve their problem? *Listening, understanding, and empathy along with honest, nonjudgmental communication.*

People act and react according to the information they receive, but sometimes this information can be misread or misperceived. Be sure you have accurate information before you make a decision. Consider the source. For example, if you watch only one TV channel, read one type of newspaper or book, or listen to only one person and believe everything he or she says, your view will be limited. You will act on the one-dimensional snapshot you have created in your mind. Instead, fully research an issue, talk to people honestly, and ask questions. Look at all sides of an issue before you decide how to act. Think of how many misunderstandings and even wars have started because of missing, partial, or wrong information.

However, even if you have reliable information and have researched the problem carefully, you may still make a mistake. Hindsight is great, but you are not clairvoyant. You have limited knowledge in the moment. Don't blame yourself for making a mistake, even though others may. Know that you did the best you could at the time. Sometimes consequences occur in our lives that we cannot predict.

Gary, a veteran, spoke of a battle he had commanded in Fallujah. Knowing the route that the enemy normally took, he split up his unit to cope with the situation. But the enemy changed its route. One group of soldiers was killed. Gary and the others had not been there to save them. The guilt of the surviving soldiers still hinders them from moving on with their lives today. Fortunately they are now meeting together on Skype to talk about the situation and process what happened. They are indeed the brave ones. I congratulate them.

If you made a mistake, or someone else did, you don't need to keep on punishing yourself or others. We are all humans and make mistakes we didn't mean to make, or regret later. Your responsibility is to admit your errors, to learn from them, and, if appropriate, to apologize. Making mistakes is part of life. It is time to forgive yourself and others and move on.

STEP THIRTEEN:
Deal with alcohol and drug addictions.

If you have chosen drugs and alcohol as a way to cope with your stress, and they are causing problems in your life, it is time to make a decision about where you wish your life to go. Although I could write pages of suggestions in this area, I won't. First of all, I am not an expert in drug and alcohol abuse counseling, and there are already several excellent books in the area that can be very helpful. Check publishers such as Hazelton and Health Communications on the Internet. Second, I believe that, rather than trying to stop on your own, you will need to join a support group that can help you turn your life around. Don't set yourself up for failure by going it alone.

Drugs and alcohol are so powerful and increase the level of dopamine (pleasure response) so much in your brain that if you are addicted, you will most likely need help to stop. Statistically, addicts make many attempts at sobriety before they succeed. If you really want to change and if you value your spouse, children and loved ones, your own life, or your job enough that you are truly willing to change rather than lose them, you need to get help.

Twenty Steps to Help You Heal

Here are a few suggestions to help you remain sober:

1. Join a support group. Tell the people in it that you are going to stop drinking and/or doing drugs. Ask for help. It's not that people have never stopped drugs on their own, but the failure rate is very high. It is easier to continue changes when you are accountable to others and you can call someone when you need support. There are great support groups for addicts. Join a twelve-step program such as Alcoholics Anonymous or Narcotics Anonymous. Choose a sponsor whom you can call day or night if you need to. Also get to know others in the group who will be there for you. The twelve steps are powerful if you work them. and they have helped millions.

If you don't have a twelve-step program in your area or prefer a different kind of group, join a VA group, church-based group for recovering addicts, or a community drug program. If you live in an isolated area, get on the Internet and search to find online recovery groups for drugs and alcohol. Join the one you think matches your needs.

2. Imagine the changes you plan to make, how you will accomplish them, and the rewards you will receive by stopping drinking and doing drugs. Take some quiet time for yourself at least twice a day. Create a new picture in your mind of what your life will be like when you stop drinking or doing drugs. Watch yourself discarding the drugs and alcohol in your house. Watch yourself saying "no" to friends who encourage you to drink, and see yourself walking away from the situation. Imagine yourself joining a group and talking to some of the people you'll meet there.

See yourself being honest about your addiction. Say out loud to yourself, several times a day, "I am an alcoholic. I am a drug addict." That will help you break your denial about your addiction. Now see yourself getting what you want, even to the details of what you look like and what clothes you will be wearing. See how happy your mate is that you are sober. Picture your children running to greet you. See the approval of your boss. Watch yourself getting the job you want. Imagining success will help your brain realize that it is possible and that you can accomplish your goal.

According to research, imagining doing something in great detail is almost as valuable as physically doing it. Olympic athletes such as skiers and swimmers, unable to physically practice right before a race, frequently use mental imaging to keep up their skills. It works!

3. Start working on changing your thinking and your beliefs. Check Step Seven on changing your thinking. As an alcoholic and drug addict, you have many mistaken ideas about life that must be changed before you can fully recover.

4. Change your behaviors. Check Step Eight on changing unwanted behaviors. Don't punish yourself with reprimands if you make a mistake, but take responsibility for your actions. Only you can change them. Never, never, never give up. Instead, praise and reward yourself every time you succeed, even though that may be only ten percent of the time at the beginning. Remember, habits are hard to break. You don't go from kindergarten to grade twelve in one day.

5. Call someone from your group and talk before you go out and use. Be honest. Slowly and surely with the help of others, old habits will lessen until the new behavior becomes the "normal one." However, whenever your stress level increases, old habits tend to return. Often they are the first way your mind will tell you to respond. For example, when you lose a job, your first thought may be, "I need a drink," or "I need some meth right now." That's natural. You have used drugs and alcohol, probably for many years, to make you feel better and help you cope. But these thoughts are far from helpful to your recovery. If a situation like that occurs, call someone immediately and talk it through.

6. Avoid places and friends who encourage you to drink or do drugs. Some people think they can return to a bar they used to frequent and keep up old friendships after they stop drinking or using. This is rarely possible. I advise you not to attend functions where large amounts of drugs and alcohol are served. Find a new group of friends who do not use, such as recovering alcoholics and former drug addicts, especially veterans' groups. They understand you and will help you remain sober.

7. Take it one day at a time. Most recovering addicts will tell you that when it comes to remaining sober, they have to take life one day at a time, sometimes one hour at a time. If they can remain sober that day, they can move on to the next day, and the next.

Brett, a veteran and former client of mine, told me early on in his recovery that he had promised himself and his girlfriend that he would never drink again. Two months later she came home to find him passed out on the sofa, a nearly empty bottle of scotch lying beside him. When it comes to addictions, making long-term promises rarely works. Lower your expectations and keep them realistic. One moment, one day, is all you have. You set yourself up for failure if you think you will never drink again.

STEP FOURTEEN:
Use your creativity.

According to recent articles I have read, many psychologists now believe that the best antidote for depression is creativity. Although this is not commonly known, creativity has been found to be a *human need*, just like food and sex. When we are creative, we feel more alive and unique than at any other time.

But even knowing these facts, we still delay creative endeavors. Why? We say, "I don't have time." Or, "It's not a priority." But maybe reframing our thoughts will help. "I'm depressed, and being creative will help me get out of this funk." Or, "Creativity is a human need and I need to be creative to feel healthy and whole. It helps me solve my problems."

As the well-known psychoanalyst Carl Jung wrote, "Often the hands know how to solve a riddle with which the intellect has wrestled in vain." During the time Jung left his mentor Freud and diverged from his teachings to develop his own theories, Jung became very depressed and spent hours at the seashore playing in the sand. He created scenes, then destroyed them and rebuilt them in different ways. Gradually his depression and anxiety lifted and he felt clear and whole again. His thinking and his feelings changed, as if by magic.

When you create something you love, you drift into an altered state and time flies. Hours pass before you realize they're gone. New ideas and solutions to problems come into your mind as though by magic. The unconscious mind finds symbolic answers for your problem without your needing to know what is happening inside. You don't need to figure things out consciously.

Creating something, regardless of whatever you decide that something will be, is a form of play and self-expression, and has been present in this world since mankind's early beginnings. Remember the ancient cave art in New Mexico, or the sculptures on Easter Island. Or the Australian aboriginal bark paintings and the Japanese sculpted gardens. Or the ancient peoples who created instruments and wrote and played music. Or designed and created clothes or houses. Or did woodworking. Or developed new food recipes. Or wrote the ancient texts we still read. Or the scientists who have spent years working on new inventions.

A couple of years ago, my husband and I visited Puerto Vallarta, Mexico. We watched as young men created large sand and rock sculptures on the beach for people to admire and enjoy until the ocean washed them away. Then they would start building again. You could see the intense enjoyment on their faces as they worked. One evening, as we set out for our walk, we noticed a group of men build a brick pathway, and we stopped to admire their work. We were amazed to listen to them discuss and decide on the patterns they would create with the bricks and sand. That pathway became a work of art, and we often heard the men laugh and sing as they laid the bricks.

I realized something important on that vacation. Anyone can find ways to be creative, even in her or his daily life and work. It all depends on how you look at something. There are endless ways to be creative, limited only by your imagination.

Here are a few suggestions for you: Use as many of your senses as you can.

1. Create art projects. Art cleanses the soul. Create your own art when you return home from overseas. You don't have to be what our culture considers a "great" artist. All you need to do is express yourself, your thoughts, your feelings in whatever medium you wish. It can be pencil, colored chalk, paint of any color and kind, and paper, or it can be wood carving, clay or metal sculpting, or sand and mud. Some people create incredible gardens or sculpt trees and bushes. Let your mind run wild. You can create forms and scenes of any kind you wish. Just let it come out of your hands into your medium. No need to have a plan or an image of what you wish to do. What comes out might be as simple as broad brush strokes of dark red and black or quiet greens and blues. Sometimes it is more powerful if you just allow your unconscious mind to do the creating.

Several American war veterans' paintings and sculptures, capturing their memories of war, now hang in the National Veteran's Art Museum. In order to deal with the horrendous memories he listened to every day while working with American war veterans, a caregiver, Bill Blahd, painted powerful scenes of war and of veterans. His art showing, "In

Our Name," is displayed in the gallery of the Linen Building in Boise, Idaho.

Russ DeVerniero, a talented, award-winning artist and a Vietnam and Panama war veteran, copes with his postwar stress by creating art and music. It has become a passion for him and has helped him deal with his anger, sleeplessness, and memories. To see or buy his art, check his website at www.seabearartstudio.com.

2. Photograph the world around you. Photography is another art form. You can take pictures of anything you wish. You can buy an inexpensive digital camera on Ebay or other websites that sell used items. Digital cameras are very forgiving, and you can erase and redo the picture as many times as you wish to get the one you want. You can photograph a person, an animal, an object, or a scene from diverse perspectives. It will surprise you how differently your favorite tree or car looks from different angles. Not only can you unleash your creativity, but because you have to concentrate fully on the scene you wish to take, you will often forget your problems and keep your mind in the here-and-now.

One veteran I met returned from the first Iraq conflict feeling very lost and depressed. When Kendrick's best friend, a nature photographer, gave him an old camera and asked him to accompany her into the forest to shoot photos, he decided to go, just for something to do. Little did he know that day would change his life. Not only was he able to spend many hours in nature, but he developed a passion for photographing wildlife, especially birds. He has won several awards and sold many of his photos, and is now hired as a photographer for outside weddings and special occasions.

3. Create music. Music is very powerful and important for many people. Create music yourself. Learn to play an instrument that you particularly enjoy and make up your own music. Try different sounds and see what nourishes you. It's fun. You can buy instruments, such as flutes and drums, for very little, or you can make your own. Used guitars are frequently on sale. When I asked a veteran how he was coping with his PTS, he said he had made a drum out of deerskin and wood and sometimes spent hours a day down by the river, drumming.

4. Write articles, a book, or poetry. You can write either fiction or nonfiction, although fiction allows you to be more creative. Create a story of anything that comes into your mind. Use your imagination and let it go free. There is no need to judge the story or grammar at this point. Just write. You can write a memoir about events that occurred in your life, or write your autobiography. But if you are writing for creativity and pleasure, focus on the times in your life you enjoyed or that were special to you. It's okay if not every scene is recorded exactly as it occurred. Your memories of the past are not completely accurate at this point, regardless how hard you try to be factual.

5. Do woodworking. Even though one veteran I know could not find a job when he returned from war, he remembered how much he had enjoyed woodworking during high school.

He built beautiful bunk beds for his two kids out of wood remaining from a neighbor's project, and carved the headboards. His kids loved them, and he felt a purpose and a new focus. Later he got a job as a cabinetmaker and installer.

6. Create a garden. For many people, gardening is one of the most engaging and satisfying projects. People who are unable to go out into the wilderness can substitute gardening to help them center and create. Grow a garden or plant some trees, shrubs, and vegetables. Watch them grow. Tend to them. They are a symbol of new life. Just placing your hands and/or feet in the earth and moving the dirt is very grounding and centering, as well as calming.

If you decide to plant a garden, create a plan and prepare the soil before you put out your plants or seeds. Plant the garden the way you wish it to be. You have the power and control in your own garden that you may not have in many other parts of your life. You can pull out the weeds, choose any plants you wish, or relocate plants to another area of the garden later if you decide you don't like your first choice. When you nurture the seeds and they begin to grow and change into mature, green, living plants, you will probably feel the same peace and joy you experience out in nature. You water and fertilize the plants and feel you are part of creation.

STEP FIFTEEN:
Have fun. Laugh. Learn to play again.

Some years ago a man named Norman Cousins wrote a book about his experience of healing from ankylosing spondylitis, which meant that the connective tissue in the spine was deteriorating. Although the doctors decided they had done everything they could to help him, he was not recovering, until he began to watch funny movies and play tapes by comedians who made him laugh. After spending a great deal of his days laughing, he recovered completely. Just as stress changes the body chemistry and reduces the immune system's ability to function, laughter bolsters the immune system to the point where the body can heal.

So have fun, play, and try not to judge yourself or others harshly. Being happy is also an emotion, and an incredibly important one to overcome anxiety, sadness, and anger. In order not to get too depressed and anxious, you need to balance those negative emotions with positive ones.

Give yourself permission to be silly, laugh, dance, goof around, tussle with your kids, mate, and friends, play games, and be a kid again. What did you love to do as a child? Or before you went to war? My father, who had PTS most of his life, rarely allowed himself to play, and he spent much of his life sullen, anxious, and depressed. He could not let go of being "perfect." His life was not a happy one, and I would not wish it on anyone.

The other day I saw a young man in his early twenties in uniform at a nearby park. Three young boys, about five years old, followed him and pounced on him. He ran after them and threw them gently on the ground. He tickled them. Then he allowed them to pin him down on the ground and tickle him. At first, all I heard were peals of laughter from the boys, but as I got closer I heard the soldier growl at them and laugh. He seemed to be having a lot of fun.

When I talked to him, he said he wasn't sure, but he might reenlist for a third tour of duty because jobs were scarce at home. For now his sister and two of her friends needed a babysitter for their boys every morning before they left for kindergarten, and he had offered to help. They were each paying him $6.00 an hour.

As I walked away, I thought how wonderful it was for those young boys to have a great male role model in their life such as this soldier. And how wonderful for the soldier to be able to let go of all the heavy responsibility he carried during his time in Afghanistan and just play and have fun for a while. I hope more men who love children will consider taking a job caring and playing with our youth when they return.

STEP SIXTEEN:
Spend time in nature.

We are all made up of mind, emotion, body, and soul, and what happens to one of these elements influences and changes the others. Spending time outdoors in nature does not only affect your body; it changes your thoughts and feelings and, for many, creates a spiritual connection. One of the veterans I talked to who had recently returned from Afghanistan told me, "I find peace when I'm out in the wilderness, and I feel safe. I wish I could get a job working there. I'd move in a minute."

Many veterans have done just that. Most of them have been severely stressed by the war. Some are working for logging companies or the forestry department, and some live far away from their families and civilization in the forest or the mountains, or on the beach. Sometimes they have a dog for companionship, but other than that, they are alone. You may have heard them called homeless veterans, mountain men, beach bums.

Why have they opted to leave civilization? Most will say they feel at home in nature. They feel secure. Everything is quiet. They fish, they hike, they climb, they hunt, they swim, they bike and canoe. Interestingly, in art therapy, when I asked veterans to draw a scene, they usually drew mountains, rocks, trees, and streams first. Then they stopped. When I asked them to add animals, they hesitated, but might add a dog, a horse, some fish, a squirrel, a deer. But when I asked them to add humans, many began to shake. Some refused. Why? Because humans are threatening. In a war zone, people are dangerous, and anyone could be an enemy.

I don't recommend that you move to the mountains or forest, but I think taking regular breaks to be by yourself in nature, or with someone you trust, is an excellent idea. Go, even if you are handicapped and in a wheelchair. Have a family member or friend take you and stay nearby if you wish to be alone. You will renew your soul. Some of my clients have said to me, "Nature is my church. I can feel close to God there."

For those of you who can, take at least one weekend a month and go camping. Fish, hike, canoe, hunt, ski, surf, or just lie under a tree or draw scenes in the sand. If you can't go to the forest, go to a park. Get away from people and the humdrum of life. It is essential to replenish your life energy.

Growing groups of veterans are turning to outdoor sports to fill in some of what civilian life does not provide. Veterans miss the excitement, camaraderie, and sense of working together as a team. Some veterans act as guides, taking groups out into the wilderness and onto lakes and rivers. Some take out adolescents and Boy Scouts. Everyone loves being in the outdoors, and it gives veterans a sense of purpose and comradeship that they miss.

Several veterans' treatment programs now take groups of veterans into the wilderness for a week or longer as a part of therapy. Wikipedia describes "Adventure Therapy" as a therapy that "approaches psychological treatment through experience and action within cooperative games, trust activities, problem-solving initiatives, high adventure, outdoor pursuits, and wilderness expeditions."

Many new programs are being launched throughout the country to help veterans transition back to civilian life. The outdoors and the team spirit nurture the veterans and prepare them to reenter civilian life. Within the group, they rebuild connections with other veterans and cooperate on projects as they did in the past (e.g., whitewater rafting). They again experience the camaraderie of a team and the thrill of the activity. Many veterans become so focused and involved in the activities that they almost forget their handicaps and their problems. In the meantime, they also learn new coping skills.

Here are the names of a few programs. Ask your local VA for any groups they can recommend. Search for "adventure therapy for veterans" on the Internet. Also check "Vets for Peace." Sun Valley Adaptive Sports in Sun Valley, Idaho, is a group that takes veterans out fly fishing. Another program called Incopah, located near Willow Creek, California, is a retreat center where veterans can reflect and recover, off grid, in the forest. Here veterans are brought back into the "tribe." Also check the Wounded Warrior Project and Kayaking Team River Runner in Fort Carson, Colorado.

The Colorado program was started by Marc Dervaes. This is Mark's advice to veterans: "Get away from the game console and into the water."

STEP SEVENTEEN:
Work with your physical body.

---

1. **Exercise daily.** Exercise helps to rebuild neurons in your brain that are particularly susceptible to stress. There are many forms of exercise, all of which help your brain release endorphins, the brain's "feel good" chemicals. Also, exercise increases muscle tone and reduces levels of stress hormone, like adrenaline. After a good workout or bout of physical labor, you will usually feel much more relaxed and happy than you did prior to exercising.

In the military, you likely spent many hours every day running, climbing, and doing pushups. Now that you are home, your body needs at least an hour a day of exercise. Even if other life changes seem overwhelming to you at this point, beginning to exercise more is a simple place to start.

It's not essential to go to a gym, and it is best to increase your exercise slowly if you have not been doing it for a while. As a beginner, don't exercise to extremes, nor to the extent that it drives your blood pressure or pulse rate too high. Run down your street or along the beach, climb a tree, lift jugs of sand, do a wheelchair race, throw balls with your kids or with a couple of friends, build a tree house, cultivate your garden, dance. Only your imagination can limit you.

Many gyms offer instruction in the martial arts. Not only are the martial arts a great way to exercise, but they also teach discipline and encourage you to feel strong and powerful again. Yoga is another form of structured exercise that includes meditation and discipline. If yoga classes are offered in your area, check them out. My son-in-law, who served two years in the Air Force, now has a black belt in three of the martial arts and attends yoga classes at least three times a week. He has a high-pressure job teaching executives around the world and often says that yoga and karate keep him sane.

2. Get enough sleep. Many veterans with PTS have difficulty sleeping. Most doctors now say that these veterans don't have a sleep disorder, but rather a hyper-arousal disorder, where their brains continuously release stress hormones such as adrenaline and cortisol into the blood and won't let them relax. Over time these increased stress hormones can actually change the brain patterns.

Why might you be over-aroused when you come home? You have spent many hours on alert, always waiting, watching, for the enemy to attack. You were never safe. If you were not ready to act at a moment's notice, you or members in your unit might have died. So your mind told you over and over again to be constantly watchful, vigilant, prepared. And during your mission, this watchfulness helped you to survive. But now you can't relax enough to fall asleep. The new learned brain pattern of hyper-arousal doesn't change suddenly now that you are home. Your unconscious mind continues to tell you that you must be on alert and that you are not safe.

For most people, sleep deprivation has very negative effects on the body, especially the brain. Veterans often say that they feel they are "going crazy" when they have insomnia. They cannot deal with even minimal stress. Small problems may send them into rages, or they may fall apart emotionally, shaking and crying. And the longer you go without sleep, the worse your problems become. You may develop high blood pressure or diabetes, or become obese. Your immune system doesn't work as well as it should and you get sick more often.

How can you begin to sleep again? Your brain will need to be retrained. You will have to learn to trust again and believe that you are safe. Changing these thinking processes takes time, so don't get discouraged. Sleep and reduced arousal are essential to health and well-being. Please see a therapist and a doctor as soon as possible for advice and/or medication.

Here are some ideas you can try to help you sleep: Experiment to find the ones that work for you.

- At least an hour before you plan to go to sleep, stop watching, reading, and doing things that excite you or that create anxiety. Change your thinking to something that helps you relax and feel secure. Watch a funny movie, read a self-help or inspirational book, listen to a relaxation CD. What you do might even be boring. My "drug of choice" is history. All I need to do is to read a chapter in a history book with all the dates and facts, and I am sound asleep.
- Find out what helps *you* relax. This may be different for each person. When your body relaxes, your

anxiety and hyper-arousal decrease. Your blood pressure and pulse rate fall. A few things that help people relax are a warm glass of milk, a cup of tea, a funny movie, relaxing music, relaxation tapes (e.g., Louise Hay CDs), a warm shower or hot bath, and deep breathing and relaxation exercises (See Step Four for suggestions.)

- Remember times you slept well and imitate that feeling. Breathe in and out, slowly and deeply. Ask yourself where you felt safe before the war, perhaps in your childhood bedroom or in your backyard. If you don't feel safe at that place anymore, where do you feel safe now? Then imagine yourself there, completely safe and relaxed. Look all around and explore the environment: what do you see, hear, smell? Relax each set of muscles from the toes to the head. Or imagine yourself floating in space or down a river toward peaceful, safe sleep. Allow yourself to drift.
- Practice safe touching. Although many people seem to be hesitant to touch others, touch is a very important part of human life from the moment we are born to the moment of death. Sexual touching is wonderful, but there are other kinds of touching as well. Safe touching is reassuring, respectful, and loving. Ask the receiver for permission to touch or hug them. Gently touching and hugging a partner, your children, your family, and your friends helps you connect and bond to each other.

Yes, touching can make you feel more vulnerable, but it can also help you relax and feel safe, supported, and cared for. Safe touching is reassuring. Snuggle in bed with your partner, or hold each other. Hold your children and let them sit on your lap. Hug a friend or relative. Safe touching cannot be faked. It must be sincere and heartfelt.

If you feel too uncomfortable just holding your partner in your arms, give each other a massage. This is a great way to meet each other's touching needs. Have your partner give you a massage on a weekly basis and exchange massages with her or him. Explore with each other. Learn how to do this in books, a class, or on the Internet. If you do not have a mate, find out if there is a massage school nearby where you can get a therapeutic massage for less cost. Get some kind of bodywork weekly if possible, especially deep body massage, to help you relax.

- Use "tapping" regularly, or as it is formally called, the Emotional Freedom Technique (EFT). Often considered to be the emotional version of acupuncture, but without the needles, EFT interrupts the emotional cycle in your body and calms the nervous system, thereby reducing your state of hyper-arousal. It helps you rebalance your energy enough to relax and fall asleep. See Step Twenty for more information about EFT and other innovative techniques.
- Change your thinking by reminding yourself that you are safe now and you are home (see Step Seven). Stop continuously running negative or worry thoughts through your mind, and learn to trust again. Think of the positive things in your life. Repeat a mantra

that helps you relax and trust, e.g., "I trust God (or substitute another word of your choice) to provide for me." You can also read quieting and positive materials to help shut down your negative thoughts. Do something non-stimulating that does not require a lot of energy from your brain and it will slow down.

- Journal and "dump" your problems. Many people, both men and women, write their thoughts and emotions in a journal before they go to bed. Journaling helps them let go of their worries enough to fall asleep. To assure that you feel safe enough to write whatever comes into your mind, keep your journal somewhere no one can find it. A small safe or a locked drawer works well.
- As mentioned earlier, exercise or work out physically during the day. If you can, take up a job or hobby that exhausts you physically.
- Don't drink coffee or anything containing caffeine for at least four hours before bedtime. Instead, drink or eat something containing tryptophan, like turkey or warm milk.
- Consider taking a vitamin, herb, or over-the-counter drug. Magnesium, vitamin B complex, L-tryptophan, melatonin, valerian root, and certain antihistamines like Benadryl, have helped many people fall asleep. Some essential oils also work. Consult an herbalist or natural food store to find out more before trying them.

- Work with your nightmares. At first you may have nightmares when you fall asleep. That's because your brain is still hyper-alert and overactive. Just keep repeating the words before you go to sleep and when you wake up, "It's okay. Dreams are not real, and I am safe." Let yourself shake after the dream (see Step Twenty). As you begin to relax more, and work through your trauma experience, the nightmares will lessen.
- Don't take naps during the day. Researchers have found that many veterans take long naps during the day and then can't sleep at night. To some degree, this is logical. During your tour of duty you had to be on constant alert, especially at night, when it was dark outside and you could not see the enemy coming.

Ed, a disabled Vietnam veteran who had fought on the front line, told me reluctantly that he couldn't sleep at night, but he could sleep during the day. So he slept much of the day while his wife was at work, and then stationed himself in his wheelchair at the front door on full alert at night. He kept his gun on his lap. With long-term therapy, medication, and the help of his wife, Ed eventually stopped taking naps and relaxed enough at night to turn his sleep patterns around.

But some veterans can sleep neither during the day nor at night. If that is you, try lying down on the sofa for a bit and relaxing during the day. Tell yourself you are safe now, and it's okay to fall asleep. No one will harm you. Over time you will begin to nap for brief periods. That's okay. Nap for a while. Let your body and your mind remember what it is like to sleep, and that it is safe to do so now.

One of the veterans, Judy, who served in the first Iraq war, came home unable to fall asleep. She spent hours roaming around in her house. She tried reading, listening to music, and watching TV, but her hyper-alert mind would not allow her to fall asleep. At night she would doze for just a moment, then suddenly jerk awake. Her body shook, her heart raced, and she wanted to scream. When I met her, she told me that she was afraid she was "going crazy" and would commit suicide. Sometimes at night she would put a loaded gun to her head.

After a month of not sleeping, she finally went to the VA for sleeping medication and anxiety-reducing drugs, then came for counseling. The drugs and counseling worked, and she was eventually able to sleep several hours a night, but still could not fall asleep on her own.

After a while she began to sleep naturally for about half an hour, but only during the day. Sometimes she would still jerk awake with nightmares. But she was thrilled to know that she could fall asleep on her own. She had felt it would never happen. Over the months she began to sleep peacefully for an hour during the day, and slowly she started sleeping at night. By the time she stopped therapy, she was still using sleeping medication, but only as needed.

3. Eat a healthy diet with conscious intention.

Over the many years that the human body has evolved, nature has determined what will keep your body and mind healthy and working to its maximum potential. What you eat and drink will nurture you or harm you. Your body will eventually succumb to diseases if you put foods, drink, and chemicals into it that nature did not mean to be there. That includes alcohol, drugs, and cigarettes.

Stress increases cortisol in the bloodstream. Research has linked this higher level of cortisol to lowered immunity and heightened depression and blood sugar related diseases, such as obesity and diabetes. So you will need, even more than others, a nourishing diet to keep your immune system and cells healthy, and the chemicals in your body and mind balanced. When you eat healthy meals you will find you have more energy and reduced anxiety, and your blood sugar levels will stabilize.

So what is a healthy balanced diet? There is no single answer. For each person it will be somewhat different. But here are a few general rules:

- As you learned in school, your diet should include fruits, vegetables (especially green vegetables), some whole grains, proteins such as nuts, beans, meat, fish, cheese, milk, and eggs, plus essential oils such as fish oils, vegetable oils, and nut oils.
- Limit refined carbohydrates such as white breads, pastries, soft drinks, and sugar of any kind. Refined carbohydrates seem to keep cortisol levels high in your bloodstream. Sugar is processed much like alcohol in the body and can create rapid mood changes and fatigue. Although sugary foods are comforting and can seem to reduce stress, they actually raise your stress hormone levels.

- If possible, eat fresh, whole, natural, and preferably organic foods. These are more expensive than processed foods but, in the long run, will keep you healthier, so you will spend less on healthcare.
- If you don't eat a healthy diet and are under stress, it is important to add a good multivitamin. Vitamin B complex, Vitamin C, and magnesium are among the first to be depleted in times of stress.

I realize that when you are under a lot of stress, it is easy to relapse into either not eating enough, or "comfort eating" and eating too much. The extra stress of shopping for healthy foods and preparing them may be more than you think you can handle. You want your life to be as simple as possible. But there are consequences to choosing the easy way out.

When I met Daniel, a veteran who had PTS, he had recently been divorced. He lived alone in a small apartment and worked for a construction company. By the time he got off work, he felt exhausted and jittery. The last thing he wanted to do was cook for himself, so each day he stopped at a fast food place for pizza or a hamburger and fries, and washed it all down with a large soft drink.

At home he felt lonely, anxious, and depressed, and missed the camaraderie of his unit. To help himself feel better, he ate several doughnuts and drank a six-pack of beer while watching TV, until he went to bed. In the morning he ate more doughnuts and drank three cups of coffee. Usually he skipped lunch.

After several months Daniel had gained weight, but what concerned him even more was that he experienced constant fatigue and frequent chest pains. When he finally saw his doctor at the VA hospital, his blood pressure, cholesterol, and blood sugar levels were high. Fortunately the dire warning of his doctor shocked him enough to take action. With the help of a nutritionist, he changed his diet. He joined a support group at the VA and decided to adopt a dog at the local shelter. Today he is a healthy, happy young man who recently met a special woman and plans to get remarried shortly.

Stress eating: The problem with stress eating is that it often becomes a habit that later is hard to break. As soon as your stress increases, you either almost stop eating or turn to food for comfort. You may crave certain foods you love. Strict diets may work for short periods, but you will tend to return to your old eating habits when your motivation diminishes or stress increases.

Here are a few tips to help you change your stress eating habits:

- Use the previous steps in this book to reduce your stress level. With reduced stress, any stress-related eating will naturally normalize.
- Change the way you look at yourself and food. Body image and weight can motivate you to diet, but the motivation usually doesn't last, and thoughts of food become obsessive and take up far too much space in your mind. It is more lasting to change your thinking about yourself and the food you eat. You may need to stay away from the mirror.

- Make your motivator good health. Learn to love, appreciate, and accept yourself. Tell yourself that you deserve and want to be healthy. Imagine yourself healthy and happy, doing what you like to do.
- Think before you put something into your body. Make a conscious decision to eat. Are you actually hungry? Will this particular food nourish you or hurt you? If you tend to be the kind of person who reduces food input dramatically under stress, make a conscious decision to eat. Even if you don't feel like eating, pick up some nutritious foods on your way home. Eat the food slowly and in small amounts, several times a day.
- It's okay to have something like ice cream or your favorite food once a day so you don't feel deprived and punished.
- Put notes on your bathroom mirror, in your car, in your bedroom, reminding yourself of your new way of thinking, and read them several times a day.
- Try conscious eating. I challenge you to try something new. Most of the time we are barely aware of what we put into our bodies. We hurry through our day and think about what we need to do next. We eat to live or eat to reduce stress. But what if we took the time and energy to become fully aware of our food and learned to enjoy every bite we ate, appreciating it in the moment? What if we became purposefully attentive to the here and now, using all our senses and noting what we experienced as we ate, and how we responded to our food? How would our body respond?

Maybe it would integrate the food more fully and use all the nutrients in it to keep us healthier. Here are a few tips to help you try this new approach:
    a. Read Step Five on self-awareness and mindfulness.
    b. Eat at least one meal a day at a place where you feel most comfortable, and where you will have no distractions such as the TV or the Internet. At work you might find a place where you can be alone and relax.
    c. Take each bite and chew it slowly.
    d. Instead of allowing your mind to wander, especially to worries, stay in the present and concentrate on your food.
    e. Use all your senses. What does the food look like, taste like, smell like and feel like in your mouth? Enjoy the flavor of the food.

In the long run, what you eat and drink is ultimately your choice. No one else can make it for you. However, remember to stay conscious in the process and make whatever you decide to put into your body a true choice.

STEP EIGHTEEN:
Rebuild your purpose in life.

VOLUNTEER YOUR TIME OR LOOK INTO GETTING A MEANINGFUL JOB.

As mentioned earlier, veterans often say that life no longer has any meaning for them after they return home. During their overseas stay, many of their decisions were of great importance and carried life-and-death consequences. But now? Feeling as if they have no purpose leads to emptiness, stress, and depression. They feel helpless, as if they have no control over their own lives, much less world events.

When I talked to Larry, an Afghanistan veteran, it was obvious he was becoming increasingly depressed since returning home. I asked him, "Have you been thinking of suicide?"

He shrugged, then said, "Why should I be alive? I have no purpose anymore. I go to work every day to a meaningless job and when I come home, my wife and kids hardly notice me. They don't need me. They're so used to being on their own."

I asked, "How did you feel when you were in Afghanistan?"

His eyes brightened and he straightened his shoulders. "Important. What I did made a big difference in people's lives. My decisions could literally save the guys in my unit or get them killed, and even the people around us, where we were stationed. I remember the day I saved a little girl from being blown to bits by an IED." His voice rose with excitement as he told the story. When he finished, he had tears in his eyes.

I said, "I noticed the change in your face and your body when you told me about saving that little girl. What was happening inside of you?"

He leaned back and nodded. "Yeah, I get it. I need to be out there doing things for others whom I can help. That's what gives my life meaning."

"Well, you can do that in a job, or you can volunteer some time for a project that you feel is important," I said.

We spent some time listing some issues he thought were important. In the long run, Larry chose to keep his job so he could help support his family and spend time with his boys, but he took one day each weekend to work at an inner city youth center or at Habitat for Humanity, building homes for poor families.

I suggest you take the time to help others who have gone through something similar to your experience. Your work does not necessarily need to help veterans, but anyone who has experienced stress after a trauma. In helping others, you may find healing for yourself.

I'm here to tell you, veterans, that we need you here at home as much as we needed you overseas. You have unique and vital skills and gifts that few other people have. Ask

yourself what skills or abilities you learned in the service that can be applied at home. Ask other veterans for suggestions as well, and write them down.

This is what I have observed: veterans like you have learned to work as teams even in the most difficult crises and places imaginable. You are strong, disciplined, and determined to persevere when others would long have given up. You are trained to be leaders and make quick decisions, especially in emergencies.

Here are some ideas to aid you in transitioning into purposefulness here at home: Some of these are paid jobs and some are not. But what do you have to lose, especially if you're not working at this point? Volunteering may even help you develop skills that will be useful in a job search later on.

1. **Rescue.** You can work in the police force or join the FBI, but also consider becoming a firefighter or emergency medical technician (EMT). More and more, as the climate changes, countries are facing emergencies such as the Haiti earthquake, Hurricane Katrina, and Superstorm Sandy. Hurricanes, tornados, and floods leave towns devastated. Fires burn miles and miles of forests and homes. Everywhere we look, it seems, people need to be rescued.

2. **Rebuild.** As big cities like Detroit are going bankrupt, buildings and infrastructure are disintegrating. Families, youth, and neighborhoods need help and support to rebuild. Habitat for Humanity builds housing for those who can't afford to build their own. Cities and counties need help rebuilding roads, sewer lines, and water lines.

3. **Feed the hungry.** People are hungry and food prices have risen precipitously. You can help collect and distribute food for the hungry. In some locales, people are banding together to find or create a space where they can recycle their organic waste into the soil and grow their own food locally. If you enjoy gardening and working with your hands, helping out in these projects will be satisfying (and you'll often get some free food as well).

4. **Teach the young.** Our youth today are floundering and need to learn discipline to know someone cares. Join a community or church youth project, the Scouts, or Big Brothers/Big Sisters to give hope to a child. Stand up for what you believe. You can be an incredible example and role model for our young people.

5. **Help a vet like yourself.** Even if you are disabled in some way, help your fellow veterans who are physically or emotionally disabled and you will help yourself as well. Join veterans' groups in your community or online. Give talks or write blogs for veterans' websites. Write articles for newspapers, or letters to the editor. Work in crisis centers and on hotlines to help others deal with their problems and emergencies.

Pat, a Vietnam veteran, only recently spoke for the first time of his war experiences and recovery from PTSD. He gave his talk to a large group of veterans and civilians on Memorial Day. As he watched the crowd, he could see that they were visibly moved by what he said. At the end of his talk, they stood up and cheered. Several recent veterans came up to him afterward to talk and ask questions. Later, Pat said that he finally felt supported by the people of America after being called a "baby killer" when he came home. He was able to release his shame and guilt of having served in Vietnam and felt he could move on. He now volunteers and helps veterans reintegrate when they come back.

Like Pat, many veterans from former wars are helping the troops who are coming home now. And so can you.

6. Influence public policy. Contact your legislators and work with them to help create jobs and better living conditions for veterans and everyone here at home. A wealthy country such as America should not have homeless and hungry veterans and children.

STEP NINETEEN:

Explore new technologies

Simulation Exposure Therapy: In 2005, Albert Rizzo, a professor of psychiatry at the University of Southern California, received a grant from the military to modify video games in order to help veterans returning from Iraq and Afghanistan cope with PTSD. Rizzo found that by immersing veterans in re-creations of combat, they could overcome the devastating patterns of avoiding anything that would remind them of their traumas. He adapted virtual reality, as we know it, into "Simulation Exposure Therapy" for service people, a type of technology that recreates virtual environments similar to those of the trauma using stories, realistic characters, and special effects to trigger the sights, sounds, and even vibrations and smells of combat, such as gunfire and smoke.

Working with a trained therapist, the veteran undergoing Simulation Exposure Therapy wears 3-D glasses to make the experience as realistic as possible. Used together with slow and methodical therapy, Simulation Exposure Therapy gives therapists a way to take combat veterans back through the actual events that have triggered PTS, in order to help them overcome their symptoms. In a small study of twenty veterans who completed eleven Simulation Exposure Therapy sessions, sixteen no longer met the criteria for PTSD after treatment. At present Barbara Rothbaum of the Department of Psychiatry at Emory University is treating veterans with exposure therapy using virtual reality plus D-Cycloserine, an antibiotic that reduces adrenaline. The treatment looks promising.

In a book called *At War with PTSD*, Dr. Robert McLay discusses what he calls, "facing the ghosts of war in a computer simulator." He claims that simulators have been used experimentally on the front lines since 2008 to immediately address PTSD reactions and reduce the risk. Although it appears that the sooner a person can face the trauma after it happens, the less likely PTSD or PTS will occur, this technique is still considered experimental.

SimCoach: While psychiatrists like Dr. Rizzo are using realistic video games to help veterans overcome their reluctance to seek help for emotional problems, visiting a clinic can still carry a stigma about being seen as weak for seeking help. For those who prefer taking a more private approach, SimCoach is a "virtual mental health guide" on the Internet that keeps all information completely anonymous, without the need to visit a clinic. With SimCoach, the virtual coach asks questions about your symptoms. When you type in your responses, SimCoach then guides you to appropriate advice and resources. Further, SimCoach is not connected to the military, so if you are a family member or loved one afraid of breaking the confidentiality of a veteran, it is a safe place to get answers.

Visit www.simcoach.org, www.braveheartveterans.org/SimCoach to meet "Virtual Vietnam Veteran Bill," a virtual character who has suffered from PTSD. While he can't diagnose your symptoms, he can give you a lot of information.

SimSensei: A newer version of the SimCoach technology SimSensei should be available this year in military bases and VA hospitals. This latest version actually senses and interprets muscle movement in the body (body language), emotional states, vocal patterns. and hand gestures to better guide the computer responses and give you, the veteran, more realistic, targeted feedback.

STEP TWENTY:
Try some special techniques.

Several techniques have been shown to be helpful for people with severe PTS, such as biofeedback, hyperbaric oxygen treatment, and Amygdala Retraining (developed by Ashok Gupta). The following are a few I have used personally and know to be effective in reducing symptoms of PTS. They are best learned with the help of a professional versed in the area. Both "tapping" and "shaking" are techniques you can continue doing on your own once you have learned them.

1. Eye Movement Desensitization Reprocessing (EMDR)
Extensive research studies have shown that Eye Movement Desensitization and Reprocessing (EMDR) is at present the most powerful and rapid technique to deal with disturbing memories of post trauma stress, panic attacks, trouble sleeping, depression, anger, and anxiety. It can bring quick and lasting relief for many kinds of emotional problems.

EMDR is a therapeutic process using right/left eye movements or bilateral physical stimulation that repeatedly activates the opposite sides of the brain. This process releases trauma memories, emotions, and negative thoughts that are caught in the nervous system, allowing people to "integrate," or create a connection between the "feelings and images" part of the brain and the logical "thinking" brain, where words and meaning reside. Many psychotherapists dealing with veterans will be well versed in the procedure.

During EMDR, the therapist will move her or his finger back and forth in front of your face. At the same time, she or he will ask you to remember your feelings and memories about your traumatic experience or a present-day event that triggered an intense reaction. You will closely track the movement of the finger, back and forth, as though watching a ping-pong ball, while recalling memories, thoughts, and feelings.

Ideally this process will help resolve the issues and rapidly decrease the negative feelings. It is most effective when used in conjunction with other techniques, such as Cognitive Behavioral Therapy (see Step Seven), ordinarily used by psychotherapists to desensitize you to your trauma. Techniques such as prolonged contact with your trauma environment, either by imagining it or actually confronting it are also frequently used along with EMDR.

2. Emotional Freedom Technique (EFT), or "Tapping"

Many of you may have heard of "tapping," and, like I, may have rolled your eyes in disbelief. Tapping different parts of your head and body while saying something? Really? But actually the technique is proving to be very effective for stress-sufferers, especially veterans and others with PTS or PTSD. Dawson Church, Ph.D., recently has conducted a number of clinical trials of EFT, the latest ones focusing on Iraq veterans who have been diagnosed with PTSD. Testing stress hormone levels before and after EFT, Dr. Church has found a considerably lowered cortisol level after EFT. Depression and anxiety are also reduced.

If you decide to try it, you will need to recall the issue and the specific trauma memory as you tap on different body meridians with your fingertips, and repeat a specific affirmation which ends in, "I deeply love and accept myself." Although I will not mention here exactly where you need to tap or what you need to say, there are great sites online that will lead you through a tapping session so that if you are unable to find a therapist who uses EFT, or are out in a rural area, you can learn it via the Internet. Some helpful sites are listed at the end of this section.

Some people call EFT the emotional version of acupuncture, but without the needles. Like acupuncture, EFT affects the body's subtle energy system and meridians. Others believe that, similar to EMDR, tapping interrupts a person's emotional cycle by confusing the brain. It tells the body to "stand down" while the brain releases the emotions and calms the nervous system, thus reducing the body's state of hyper-arousal and rebalancing energy.

EFT practitioners believe that the cause of all negative emotions is a disruption in the body's energy system, and that trauma is retained at a cellular level. Regardless of when your trauma occurred, the data is still stored inside your cells, and the memory is trying to protect your body from being traumatized again. EFT helps you clear these cells and return them to normal.

There are several amazing stories online of veterans recovering from PTSD with the help of EFT. A Vietnam veteran whom I know personally had suffered from severe PTSD since his war experience forty years ago. He had been in therapy for years and had used several drugs for anxiety, nightmares, flashbacks, and inability to sleep until a year ago, when he finally consulted a therapist who used EFT. Although, like all veterans with PTSD, he longed to be free from his pain, he had little faith in the technique itself. He told me that he had tried too many "cures" to believe any would actually work. But EFT did work. Now he taps daily, and sometimes many times a day, when he begins to feel anxious. At present he is off all medications and enjoys what he calls a "normal" life.

Tapping, like other techniques, can be learned on your own, but for maximum effectiveness, you should learn it from a practitioner who specializes in the technique.

Here are some websites I have found helpful:

- tryitoneverything.com
- emofree.com (the site of Gary Craig, founder of EFT)
- thetappingsolution.com by Nick Ortner. The website gives free information and films for veterans.

3. Tension and Trauma Release Exercises (TREs), or "Shaking"

As I mentioned earlier, shaking is one of the body's natural responses to trauma or severe fright. Animals do it, children do it, and adults do it. However, many of us have grown up thinking that to show fear is to acknowledge we are weak, so we try our best to stop our bodies from doing what they would naturally do to release the energy from the trauma.

We hold the stress inside our bodies and muscles, where it creates pain, emotional tension, and illness.

Of course, during battle you are not able to stop after an attack and take the time to shake, so tension remains stored in the body, to be released in the future. But in most situations you will probably not take the time to shake on purpose later, when you are alone and relaxed. When the discharge of energy doesn't occur, the brain translates this tension into intense emotions such as rage and shame.

Several years ago, after experiencing a severe trauma, I found my body automatically jerking and wanting to shake whenever I started to relax. At first I restrained my body. But then I realized that if I gave my body permission to jerk and shake for a while, I felt relieved and much less stressed. So I started to shake for about twenty minutes a day before I went to bed. I was amazed at the difference it made in the way I felt, both emotionally and physically.

Dr. David Berceli first developed a specific shaking technique to release stress and trauma from the body while working with people immediately or shortly after natural disasters and political violence in various countries. These tension and trauma release exercises have been shown to be very effective with military personnel as well. At present these special techniques are taught in workshops or by therapists all over the country and in several areas of the world. Check www.traumaprevention.com and www.Landonwerks.com for information.

If you don't have access to learning this technique, lie down on your back on the floor. Take several deep breaths and then imagine seeing a dog shake after a trauma. Give your body permission to shake, understanding that it's a normal process that our bodies have developed over a very long time to release excess energy after a frightening experience. If it feels uncomfortable for you to shake in front of others, do the shaking in private.

Conclusion

And so we come to the end of the steps of the ladder to recovery. I sincerely hope this book has helped you on your journey to healing, hope, and a more fulfilling life. No one can conclude this book better than Patrick Overton, the Vietnam veteran who wrote in his poem:

The Healing Wall

I left the Wall
I ascended from that deep hole.
Tired, emotionally exhausted,
I looked back where I had been.
I knew my pain had not magically left me –
I carry it with me today –
but I carry it, it no longer carries me.
This was the healing I could not find before –
The Wall told me my name was not there
and said, "Go live your life, you do not belong here."
And so I do, live my life now, beyond the Wall.

PART THREE

Families and Friends

Widows' Song

He did not come back,
That scarred half-man
In a wheelchair who stares
At nightmares I cannot see
And, asleep, screams in the night.

by Linda Farrell Erickson

Introduction to Families and Friends

While I was working as a therapist, and also while I was writing this book, I talked to many family members and close friends of veterans. Invariably they asked me how they could help their loved ones. Recently I met with a friend who had married a Vietnam veteran while he was in the midst of his war trauma. He had been diagnosed with PTSD about eight years after the war.

I knew that both partners had years of therapy, together and alone, and were now doing well in the relationship, so I asked Rachel how their marriage had survived all these years.

She looked at me, sighed, and said, "Patience, unlimited patience."

We talked for a while and then she said, "You know, I had to learn to not take what he said or did personally, or I'd be hooked into an argument that fast." She snapped her fingers.

I asked her what she thought was her husband's major issue during those years.

"Control," she said immediately. "Major control issues. When he felt he wasn't in control, he would go crazy. He'd yell and throw things."

Before we parted I asked her what she had learned in all these years and whether I could include some of her story in this book.

"Yes of course. It's really hard at times to live with someone who has PTSD, and I think the families need all the help they can get. I've grown so much. I am a much wiser person now. But I wouldn't try to fool anyone by saying it was easy. I guess I learned how to listen, empathize, and not react. And when I couldn't handle it, I had to remove myself without blaming myself for having done it wrong. I don't know if we would have made it without both of us being really committed and willing to change. I often think I should start a group for the families and friends of veterans."

I nodded my head. "That's a really great idea. There are so many veterans who have returned recently and will return soon. The families desperately need to meet and talk."

She looked me in the eyes. "Anna, you grew up with a father who suffered a lot from war and you know what the family goes through. How about you? You need to write about that."

I thought about what she said for a long time. And that's when I decided to write Part Three of this book. My list isn't complete or in great detail. Many of you no doubt can add to it, but it includes some of my ideas and the ideas of several of my clients, mothers, fathers, wives, partners, and friends who were in similar situations as you are.

I recommend you read the entire book but particularly Part One about Post Traumatic Stress, and also the first two steps in Part Two of the recovery program, before you read the following suggestions for family and friends. Many of the strategies will be effective for you as well.

I refer to the family and friends of the veteran as "you" and to the veteran as "he" in most cases, but it is meant to apply to both sexes.

What you can do to help the veteran you love.

My father lived most of his life with Post Traumatic Stress (PTS). When triggered, he would spend months in what is now known as PTSD, a "disorder." My mother, my sister, and I suffered as well, but my sister and I never knew why until much later. "That's just the way Dad is," we'd say. Years ago it was not acceptable for a man to talk about his emotions and his pain, or show them in any way, or talk about the horrifying events that he had experienced. And my mother encouraged my dad's silence. Fearing his terror and intense anger, she would say, "It's no good remembering. It just makes it worse."

Regardless of how hard my father tried to repress his past, I could tell when he remembered. He would scream out in the middle of the night and walk the floor. During the day he became withdrawn, anxious, and depressed. Sometimes he would not speak to us for days. Then he would burst into uncontrollable rages. During those times I was afraid he would commit suicide. When people mentioned some important event in the future, he would say, "I won't live that long." He lived to be eighty-eight. When my sister and I made plans, Dad would become sullen and try to dissuade us. "You never know what's going to happen," he would say. "We might not live that long."

As a child I knew something was wrong, but having no idea what that something was, I thought his problems must be my fault. I watched his every action and reaction and tried to please him and "make him feel better," but regardless of how hard I tried, I was never "good enough" to take away his pain.

Unaware of the pain and the patterns my father had learned in war, I passed too many of them on to my own children. The experience of living with a father who never resolved his PTSD damaged my self-esteem, confidence, and zest for life for many years, until I worked with PTSD survivors and discovered how to help myself as well as them. I wanted passionately to help people like my father resolve their issues and live normal happy lives. That way they would not pass on the consequences of their trauma to their children. In most cases, together with my clients, we succeeded.

When I asked family members and close friends what they saw as veterans' main issues, invariably they agreed with my friend, Rachel. "Control. Veterans need to feel they have control over their lives."

That's logical, when you think of what veterans have experienced in war. Their lives and their "brother's and sister's" lives were never safe. Within a second the enemy could kill or maim all of them. They carried their guns everywhere so that they could protect themselves and the others in their unit. Even today, many veteran's always carry a gun. It is a symbol that states, "I am safe and I am in control of my life."

Untreated PTS and PTSD in veterans affects the entire family. You are the ones who usually first notice and feel the withdrawal, the isolation and the anger of your loved one. You are on the receiving end of these angry, guilty, paranoid, and explosive feelings. You may be afraid for yourself and your children. You may be seeing your loved one abuse alcohol and drugs and causing family disruption. PTS often causes your loved one to shut down or become numb, and you are left without the person you and the children once knew and need.

Here are some things you can do to help your loved one:

1. **If you are a mate, a family member, or friend, plan how you can help your loved one reenter your immediate family and extended family.** If you are a close friend and have had a group of friends previous to the veteran's military service, plan how you can help the veteran reenter the group.

REENTRY:

- Lower activity levels initially. When you are together, unplug the phone and focus on each other.
- If you have children, arrange for relatives or friends to keep them for a few days after they've seen and spent a little time with their father or mother.
- Try to create the flavor of a get-away vacation, but keep it simple and as stress-free as possible.
- Cater to your loved one. Cook favorite foods, listen to favorite music, watch favorite TV shows, or do anything you know or learn your loved one enjoys.

Ask, don't assume. His likes and dislikes might have changed while he was gone.
- If you are partners, pace yourself with sexual intimacy. Explore slowly and learn to know each other again.

2. Be patient. Decrease your expectations. Especially if veterans have had several tours of duty, they feel they are entering an alien world when they return. After the immediacy of war and always being on alert, veterans don't know how to let down and reintegrate. Some of them say they feel as though they are addicted to the adrenaline rushes, and now the drug is gone. Some even say that they know inside that they create drama in their lives to bring back that rush. Remember, changes take time. Often a long time. You may think he or she is improving, but then the symptoms get worse again. Forward and backward. Lower your expectations, but don't give up. Usually the relapses occur less frequently over time.

A person with severe stress after trauma may need to talk about the trauma over and over again. This is part of the recovery process and lessens the charge in the emotions over time. (Check Step Eleven on memories in Part Two.) Let your loved one talk, rather than telling him to stop going over the past and move on. If it is too difficult for you to listen to his war experiences try to convince him to see a counselor.

3. Give him reassurance, love, and compassion. When veterans come home with severe stress after their trauma, they are often easily startled. They are afraid for their safety.

Reassure him that he is home now and he is safe. Be careful not to surprise him.

Appreciate who he is. What did you love about him or her before the war? That person is still there somewhere inside. Veterans very much need loved ones to be on their sides. Reassure him that you love him and will stick by him (but only if that is true) and you'll work things out together. Read Part One in this book and other books about veterans' experiences so you can place yourself into the veteran's "shoes." When you can allow yourself to feel and understand what it would be like to go through similar experiences, then you can become truly compassionate.

4. Be fully aware. It is essential for you to read Part One about the nature of PTS and PTSD, so you know exactly what to look for and what to expect. It is much easier to remain calm inside if you know that what happens is part of the syndrome of PTS and not something specific to him. Many people around the world who have experienced severe trauma will react similarly. Also remember that PTS is largely a physical disorder and your loved one is not intentionally trying to hurt you.

If you are concerned that your loved one is withdrawing and has become hopeless and depressed, you are probably afraid he or she might commit suicide. Your loved one does not want to die. He wants the pain to stop. Take any talk of suicide seriously, even if it was said in a joking way, especially if he carries a gun at all times. Ask him questions in a gentle way. If the depression persists, tell him you will make an appointment for him at the Vet Center or the VA. Make the appointment and take him to his appointment. If he refuses, there isn't much you can do except see a counselor yourself and ask for advice. He is an adult and can make up his own mind. If he attempts suicide, call the police. It is essential for him to get help, but if something happens, don't blame yourself. Sometimes veterans show no signs of what they are planning.

5. Ask, don't assume. Ask what he needs from you, what he likes, what he wants to do, and what is too much for him to do. If he has nightmares, flashbacks, or outbursts, sit down during a calm time and work out together what you can do and what the children or others can do that would be helpful to him. Read Part Two, Step One on becoming stable to give you some ideas.

6. Listen and empathize. Although you may believe you have the answers to his issues, give no advice unless he asks for it. If you hound him, he, like anyone else, will get angry and rebel. You can suggest something to him, but then let it go. If he doesn't take your suggestion, know that most of the time he isn't quite ready to take that step. It has nothing to do with you personally. So just listen to anything he wants to talk about, including what happened during the war. And if he refuses to talk, encourage him, but don't push too hard. Let him come out on his own, but let him or her know that you are there when or if he wants to talk. Place no judgment on what he says, unless it is about harming himself or someone else. Then you must act.

If you don't feel you can listen to details of the war stories, help him seek counseling or a VA group where he can speak freely and be understood. My mother could not handle my dad's war experiences, and he learned to be quiet and keep all his feelings inside. He carried the trauma with him all his life. Don't be afraid of his feelings. Feelings come and go and are normal. So unless he becomes violent or hysterical, it's okay for him to be angry or to cry. Most veterans will need to face their emotions sooner or later.

7. Don't take what he says or does personally. Not taking your loved one's actions and feelings personally is a big challenge, especially when the person blames you, withdraws, or yells at you. Remember that it may have more to do with his symptoms of PTS than anything you have done. Here is a way many people have learned to be able to remove themselves emotionally at that time. Picture yourself standing away from the scene, maybe on a hilltop, watching what is going on. Become a rational, not emotional, adult. Remind yourself that getting emotionally involved will only rush both of you full force into battle or into depression.

When I went into the field of psychology, I learned two ways to defuse anger. They have worked well for me over many years. As a matter of fact, I talked down a Vietnam veteran who was pointing a gun at me once, using these techniques. He had abused his wife several times and blamed me for her finally leaving and going to a shelter.

- Take some of the blame and apologize for what you can honestly see as your part in the problem. Don't give excuses at this point. Come up with a solution. For example, "I can see you are feeling pretty frustrated right now. I'm sorry. You are right that I have not been spending enough time with you. Would it be okay if we sit down tonight and come up with some ways to change that?" In the evening, sit down and talk about ways both of you can change what is going on. Make sure you carry out your part of the plan.

- Ask several logical and pointed questions about his complaints. Use an adult, non- emotional voice. "Could you tell me exactly what you mean by not spending enough time together? How much time do you think we should spend together? What can I do to help make this problem better?"

8. Include your loved one. Reintegrate him into your lives, but don't expect him to resume his life as it was before the war. Much has happened. Include him in whatever he can handle and is willing or interested in doing. Be realistic, but expect as much functioning as possible.

If you are partners, have a date night once a week so you can get to know each other again. If you have children and limited money, form a babysitting group that exchanges time. Do things together you both enjoy. When you go out, focus on the things you love about each other. Be honest but not hurtful.

Suggest going out to coffee or to a picnic in the park with the kids or friends, take a hike together, go to a football game outside, rent a funny movie, or have dinner with a few friends at your house. Restaurants and places with a lot of people can be very stressful for those with PTS. I'm sure you can think of a lot of other things you can do.

9. Allow the veteran as much control as you can without hurting you or others. Veterans are often afraid of not being in full control of their lives. They were very aware that they were never safe during the war. And if they weren't in control of everything, terrible things could and would happen. Of course, logically you know no one really has control over his or her life. You don't have control over the world, like weather or earthquakes, and ultimately you don't have control over other people's feelings, thoughts, and actions. You have control only over your own, and sometimes only tentatively. When veterans return, that feeling of the need to control everything in their lives to feel safe again does not automatically go away. It may take a long time.

Back off as much as possible. And how can you do this? By changing your thinking and behavior. (Check Part Two, Step Seven.) I counseled a client who had a difficult time allowing her husband to do some of the things she thought were controlling of her and her kids when he returned home. She would get angry, leave, and slam the door behind her. That behavior triggered a cycle of anger and withdrawal in her husband. She wanted to change her reaction.

One day she came in and said that she had finally come to peace with a lot of his controlling behaviors. What she now said to herself was, "In the light of eternity, how much does this matter?" Most of the time, she realized that most of his behaviors didn't really matter very much. When they did, she addressed them calmly.

10. Work out your roles again. If you have children, you have no doubt taken on the role of other parent while your loved one was gone. You may have decided to add a second job during his absence, plus keep all responsibilities for the home and children. In many situations, your children may have taken on more adult roles and more responsibilities as well. Now that the veteran is back, he may feel left out and want to return to his former position in the family. You and the children may have difficulty shifting these responsibilities back to the veteran and may feel uncomfortable or even angry at the disruption to your family system. That's normal. The adjustment is often a difficult one and needs to be worked out together in family meetings or in couples' or family therapy with the help of a counselor or chaplain.

11. Deal with trust issues. Do you trust your spouse (or son, brother, or friend) at this point? You may feel distant from each other, as though you don't know the person who has returned. You can see he has changed, but you don't know how he thinks, what he wants and needs. Make sure you are honest (in a kind way) about your feelings and what you think. Then act on your words. You don't trust someone who says one thing and then does another shortly after. Remember, love is freely given, but trust is earned.

Veterans are often afraid of touch at the beginning. A little voice inside tells them touch is dangerous and it startles them. Always alert them and make sure they are comfortable with you touching them. If you are partners, you will need to deal with sexual issues. Sometimes a partner doesn't trust that the other person has been loyal to him or her. Acknowledge the issue and talk. If your needs and desires have changed, let the person know. But if you can't come to an understanding with each other, seek help.

12. Keep stress to a minimum in your lives if possible. People who are already severely stressed do poorly with increased stress in their lives, but don't be so concerned about it that it disrupts your life or your family's life. For instance, don't start arguments about things you know will trigger the veteran, or go out and buy expensive new clothes when you have very little money. If there are problems you know will be very stressful for your loved one, but need to be addressed, it is better to have a third party, such as a minister or counselor, help you deal with the issues together. Be optimistic and think positively. Encourage him to go to VA group meetings or to go out into nature, where he can relax.

13. Bring laughter, enjoyment, and humor into your lives. Laughter decreases the stress hormones in your body and changes your outlook on life. Sit down together, if possible, and talk about what you both would like to do to bring laughter into your lives. Watch funny movies or TV shows, especially before bedtime so as not to trigger nightmares. Do activities that you both enjoy and that make you laugh. Take time with friends who like to have fun. You can go boating, fishing, skiing, or play games together. Go to the gym together or play tennis. Read funny books or comic books together. Turn work into play and kid around.

Sometimes when someone is depressed, a little distraction helps. Creating something together you both like doing, or encouraging him to find a creative outlet such as gardening, art, music, woodworking or anything else you know he enjoys, will change his hopelessness thoughts and yours, too. (Check Part Two, Step Fourteen and Fifteen, for some ideas.)

14. Ask your loved one what he needs from you. Then let your loved one know what you need from him. After a long absence, he has no more knowledge of what you need than you have of what he needs. Yes, you knew each other before the war, maybe for many years, but he has changed since then and so have you. Sit down over a cup of coffee and begin to talk. Ask him what you can do to help him reintegrate into this new world. Then let him know how he can help you. Keep your requests realistic and simple. If he is suffering from severe trauma, he may only be able to help you with your most urgent needs, such as giving you a warning that he is very angry or that you are stepping over the line he must draw to feel okay. A code word that you agree on, such as "red," will often work for both of you.

15. Look underneath the aggression and drug problems. As I have mentioned earlier, aggression usually comes out of the veteran's fear of loss of control in his life. Drugs stop the emotional pain and release a lot of dopamine in the brain so he feels good. If the veteran in your life becomes aggressive, either physically or verbally, first of all, try to talk him or her down. But if that doesn't work, leave the situation if you can. Instead of merely looking at the actions, see who your loved one really is, not connecting it to his behaviors. Ask yourself what he may be afraid of. In most cases he is dealing with the fear of not having control. This triggers his feelings of helplessness, and he automatically reverts to instinct mode. Some veterans will do almost anything to feel in control again, even to the extent of intimidating and manipulating you. Try to settle your conflicts in a logical and nurturing way. If you can't accomplish this on your own, seek couples' counseling.

If he is an addict, encourage him to go to counseling, or to Alcoholics Anonymous or Narcotics Anonymous. You may need to attend Alanon meetings to learn how to deal with him and the situation.

16. Try to anticipate and prepare for your loved one's PTS triggers. Observe him and note what you see that triggers him. Talk about what triggers him and ask him what you and/or the children can do to help him. Common triggers are things that remind the veteran of the trauma of war. Usually they are people or places, sights, sounds, smells, even the tastes of war. The smell of gun smoke and the sound of gunshots are common ones. Check Part One and Part Two, Step One, to learn more about triggers and symptoms of PTS. When the triggers occur, you will know what to expect and you will be prepared to support him.

17. Set boundaries and enforce them consistently. Sometimes veterans need motivators to change behaviors especially if they have become addicted to drugs and/or alcohol. Sudden rage and violence are other behaviors very difficult for veterans to stop. It is as important for the veteran as it is for you to set a line that can't be crossed. When both of you are calm, let him know quietly what that line is and what will happen if the line is crossed.

For instance, you might say, "No physical or emotional violence will be allowed or tolerated with the children or me." You must decide what the consequences will be if it occurs. You may decide that you and the children will leave immediately for an hour to let your loved one calm down. You might call it a time-out. When you are both calm again, get back together and talk. Work out a word that he can say when he feels you are acting in such a way as to trigger him, or that you can say when he is getting close to that line. It might be something like "red light" or "stop," or a code word that works for both of you.

If the behavior does not change, ask him or her to come to therapy with you. If he refuses to go to therapy, make an appointment for yourself before you decide on a divorce. But if he continues to be violent with you or the children, you must take a time of separation until the behavior has changed. Veteran's parents, family members, and friends, need to ask him to find another place to live until his behavior changes. You and the rest of the family deserve to be safe.

18. Encourage him or her to go for counseling, either alone or with you. There is usually a VA or the Vet Center close enough for the veteran to attend. As I mentioned in the introduction, according to the VA, nine times out of ten, it is a family member or a loved one who encourages the veteran to seek help when he is suffering from PTS. Veterans rarely seek help on their own. If you are having relationship issues, ask him to come to couples' counseling with you.

For therapy to be effective in the long term, *both* of you must want the relationship to improve and *both* must be willing to change. Without this prerequisite, couples' counseling rarely works. *You* can make changes, but you have no control over *his* actions. All you can do is warn him you will leave if his behavior does not change. However, I don't recommend you threaten to go unless you are absolutely sure and ready to leave. You need to have a plan in place before you leave. Check for places you can stay, etc. Seek out individual counseling for yourself first.

19. Encourage your loved one to return to school, sports, drama club or social clubs. Also encourage all creative endeavors. These activities can help veterans overcome their depression. See Step Fourteen

20. Encourage the community, friends, and families to hold public welcome back ceremonies. Native American tribes hold welcome back rituals for their warriors and help them integrate back into society. Come up with your own celebration and ritual to welcome your loved one back. Check Step Ten.

21. Ultimately you will need to let go. I'm not saying you will have to leave, or that you must stop loving the person. I'm merely reiterating that you can't change another person or that person's behavior. You can only change yourself. The twelve-step programs like AA and Alanon have a wise saying that states, "Let go and let God." Lean back and trust. Another word people often use is *allow*. Allow him the opportunity and the right to choose how he wishes to live his own life. If he is violent to you and your children and he doesn't change, I recommend that you separate and get counseling.

What you need to do to take care of yourself.

Most of the steps for veterans in Part Two of this book can help you as well as your loved one, so after you read this list, check them also. Although these steps have been written for veterans, they apply to most people under severe stress. Select the ones you need and skip those that don't relate to you.

In addition:

1. **Balance your life.** Many family members say it is exhausting to continuously be available and attentive to their emotionally and/or physically injured loved one. It is exhausting to always be "nice" and to serve someone else. Caretakers have very little time for themselves. Eventually they tend to become depressed, anxious, and ill.

Remember, you are not a robot. You are a human being with feelings, thoughts, and a body that needs restoring. So it is essential to balance taking care of yourself and your loved ones. Take an hour or so each day for yourself that has nothing to do with taking care of someone else or with working. The time must be spent on something you want to do, something that nurtures and renews you, even if it is as simple as reading a book you enjoy or taking a nap. Maybe you like to take a walk in the park by yourself and watch the sunset, or spend some fun time with one of your friends. Maybe you like reading books, or gardening, or doing yoga.

One woman I know, who is married to a veteran with Alzheimer's disease, has asked three of her husband's friends to help her. One spends two hours with her husband on Monday, another on Wednesday, and another on Friday. The plan has allowed her to go out for periods of time, take classes, go to the gym, and join a yoga group without worrying about him. She says it has kept her sane.

2. Get involved in projects that excite you and bring out the creative side of you. Read Part Two, Step Fourteen. Being creative often helps stop depression and makes you feel alive. It is actually a need humans have, just like eating. Maybe you like to sing. Join a choir. Or paint. Take a class. Or act. Join a theater group in your area. Or write. Join a writers' group. Or do photography. Or watch birds. Follow your interests and find new things that excite you. Experiment. Find something that, when you do it, you will lose all sense of time.

3. Reconnect Spiritually. Read Part Two, Step Ten. Connecting with God or whatever you call that power in the universe greater than you, can renew your hope and give you peace even in the most difficult times. Do your spiritual practice, meditate, and/or pray each day when you wake up or before you go to bed. It may be a short time or as much as an hour. Start by thanking God for all the good things you have in life. Your husband, wife, son, or friend is alive and with you today. That's a gift. You live in a democratic country of plenty. Giving thanks is a way of changing your perspective of the day ahead of you.

4. Take time to journal each day. Many of my clients have said that journaling was the most important technique they used to get through difficult times. Often they felt they could not speak to other people about what was going on inside of them, but they could release their feelings and thoughts onto paper. It helped them let go of their worries, anger, fears, and guilt. If you don't want anyone to read your journal, you may wish to take it to work. Keep it somewhere safe. If you wish you can burn the pages after you have written them. Burning those thoughts and feelings can actually symbolically help you let them go.

5. Exercise and eat healthy foods. Check Part Two, Step Seventeen. When you are under stress it is often easiest to "veg out" in front of the TV or stop at a fast food restaurant for dinner. But in the long run, doing so daily will create more problems in your life. People who are stressed need more vitamins, especially the B vitamins. So take your vitamins daily and eat a healthy diet of vegetables, fruit, and protein. Keep your meals simple if you don't want to spend time and energy cooking. Substitute fruit for dessert and snacks.

Create an exercise program that you can do daily, even in front of the TV in the evening if you wish. I am not fond of doing exercises. I think of them as boring, so for me it is important to have some distraction in order not to avoid them. Having my husband read to me, watching TV, or walking or running outside in a beautiful area, such as a park or the forest, helps.

6. Change your thinking and behavior. Empower yourself and become resilient. Read Part Two, Steps Three, Seven, and Eight. Family members and close friends often begin to think more and more negatively, depending on how their loved ones are doing. You begin to feel like a yoyo and you lose yourself. *He's doing well today. I'm doing well today. He's doing poorly today. I'm doing poorly today.* Remember, you are not the other person and you are not responsible for his problems or his actions. He is. You can be willing to help, but you can't make somebody change. You can only be responsible for you, and you can only change your own thoughts and your behavior. The rest you will have to let go.

7. Have an alternate plan. You and your children have a right to be safe. If you are not safe, call the police or 911. Leave the house if you can. If he refuses to get help and change, and remains violent with you or the children, you will need to take the children and leave, at least until he gets help. Call the Battered Women's Network if you have nowhere to go or you have no money. I suggest that any partner who has a potentially violent mate obtain his or her own credit card or keep enough cash somewhere safe, in case he or she must leave. The same advice is important for friends and for parents who take in their loved one after he returns from war. If the veteran becomes violent with you or another family member, you may need to have him move out of your home. Ask for a restraining order, if necessary.

If the veteran is abusive physically or verbally, seek counseling immediately and make it a stipulation for staying with him. You should never feel as though you deserve to stay where you are being abused. If both of you are willing to deal with the issues, there is a high likelihood that the marriage or relationship can work. Don't stay with a person who abuses the kids, period. Children are vulnerable and not capable of defending themselves. It is your job as the adult to keep them safe as much as is possible. In order for you to return, he must get help first and actually be willing to change.

8. Seek counseling if you need help making decisions, or when you need to talk to someone confidentially. The VA and Vet Center provide counseling for family members as well as veterans. If you are concerned about confidentiality and you have your own health care, you might wish to go to a counselor of your choice outside the system. A counselor can help you deal with your own issues and can advise you on how to take care of yourself. He or she can also help you work out the lines you must draw in your relationship to feel good about your life. Is it okay for your loved one to drink or do drugs? How much is okay? When do you say no? You may have some friends you can talk to, but make sure you can trust them to keep what you say confidential. Can they listen, be objective, and be realistic and rational instead of merely emotional?

9. If you feel overwhelmed by all you have to do, take time to write a list and prioritize it. Read Part Two, Step Three, on empowering yourself. At the end of the day or the week, you will find that you will probably not have been able to complete all the items on the list. Make a new list. Instead of worrying about the things you didn't get done, look at all your successes. What did you get done? How might this change your life for the better? Maybe you made an appointment to see a therapist. That's a giant step forward.

10. **If possible, attend group meetings with other partners or family members of veterans.** Usually the VA or your closest Veterans' Center will have a group meeting for families, but if none is available in your area, form a group yourself. The VA can help you find others who would be interested. Another option is to attend Alanon, a twelve-step program for codependents, located in or near your town. Their number will be in your telephone book or on the Internet. Call them and see what they offer. Go to a couple of meetings before you say it's not for you.

You can also look into Internet-based groups consisting of veterans' families and friends and join them. Although meeting face-to-face with other members may be the most ideal way to function as a group, the Internet can be very valuable when you don't have access to a physical group. It may also be that you are a person who would rather speak to a stranger about confidential matters than someone in your own area who might know you or your loved one. Or it may be that, because of your situation at home, you can't leave the house to attend meetings.

11. **Don't be afraid of your emotions.** Read Part Two, Step Nine, about dealing with emotions. You are human, and part

of being human is having emotions. They are normal and are not "bad." They are merely feelings. They are energy in motion and will come and go. It's how you *act* on them that counts. When you are angry, do you lash out at people, or do you go out and mutter to yourself or scream at the sky as you run or exercise to get rid of the energy?

Yes, family members feel anger at what is going on, and that's natural. They are often angry that the VA takes much too long to help them financially or otherwise, that the war has left the returning veteran helpless and now without a job, that you must take responsibility for everything, and that others don't understand. I'm sure you can add a lot more reasons to be angry.

Underneath that anger is often fear. Fear of loss. Fear of the future. How are we going to live? Will he ever be able to work again and get a job? Will my loved one always be as emotionally and physically stressed as he is now? Will he ever stop drinking?

But with the anger and fear is often a feeling of deep grief. A common sadness that families speak of is the grieving for the persons they once knew and who may never return; the grieving of lost expectations; of how they thought their lives with the veterans would be when they returned; and for the hardship they face every day.

If you are feeling any of the emotions I have mentioned, it is not because you are weak. Your problems are real and your feelings are normal. But if you hold all your feelings inside and pretend they don't exist, it is likely that in time they will multiply to such a degree that they will harm you not only emotionally, but also physically. Please get help and do some of the exercises I have listed in Step Nine, so you can release those feelings in a healthy way.

12. Accept yourself, with all your faults and limitations. Check Part Two, Steps Eight and Ten. You are human like the rest of us on this planet. You will make mistakes. In order to reduce the stress in your life and feel at peace, you must learn to accept yourself and love yourself. That doesn't mean that you can do anything you wish and continue that negative behavior and still feel good about yourself, but that you must learn to forgive yourself for what you have done, honestly apologize, and work on changing your behaviors. Then move on, instead of dwelling on your mistakes and feeling guilty. **You deserve a good life.**

What your children need.

This vitally important section should be a complete book in itself. But because of limited space, I have merely included a few pointers. Look into other resources, too, such as parenting books, child development books, and the Internet for more help, or talk to a counselor who works with children to get advice. Join a group for parents or for families of veterans, if available in your community or church. If not, check the Internet for such groups. You will receive both good advice and empathy from people in similar circumstances.

A third of all children who have a veteran or soldier as a parent experience emotional problems. Depression, anxiety, and acting-out behaviors are common. Your veteran loves the children as much as you do, and he does not wish to hurt them in any way, but as with my father, it is inevitable that the children will be affected. Grandparents, if your son or daughter is not willing to talk to the children about what is going on, please take time to do so. No children deserve to grow up thinking that their parents' negative feelings and actions were their fault.

1. **Talk to the children about the veteran's behavior (such as flashbacks and nightmares) and the reasons why he is acting the way he is.** Explain rationally what is happening. Young

children believe that they are the center of the universe, so if things are not going right, it must be their fault. An adolescent will often feel very angry and may act out or become anxious and depressed. This is not the dad he or she knew. He is no fun. Or he is mean and controlling and mistreats mom. Will my parents get a divorce?

Most of the time children are not aware of what is going on inside of them. They have no idea why they are feeling so angry, or why they can't concentrate, or why they are depressed. Typical acting-out behaviors include stealing, skipping school, neglecting homework, getting bad grades, fighting, withdrawing and isolating from family and friends, and doing drugs and alcohol. Look at Part Two, Step Two for some other suggestions for dealing with the children.

2. Let the veteran tell the kids what would be helpful to him, especially during flashbacks, rages, or times of withdrawal. Talk to your children together. If your spouse is not willing to be part of the discussion, talk to them alone. Talk to all the children, even the young ones, who will pick up the energy around you and the rest of the family.

When my youngest child was not yet of school age, I had a severe attack of arthritis. and I'm sure I was not always pleasant to be around. My son and his friend often played at our house. They were attempting to be grown-up by getting their own drinks from the refrigerator. You can guess what happened. Each time they spilled grape juice onto the floor, I would get upset, and they would run and hide.

Recently my son and I talked about the incident. He remembered it and told me that both he and his friend had thought they were very naughty for spilling things. I said, "It wasn't because you were being bad that I got angry at you. It was because I had arthritis and I hurt a lot every time I had to bend down and wipe up the juice." I could see the relief in his face as he said, "Why didn't you tell us mom? It would have made a huge difference."

3. Tell them what they can do to avoid triggering the veteran. Let them know in simple terms what is happening, what war is about, and why their father or mother has the symptoms she or he has at present. Emphasize that it is not their fault. Then, together with the veteran if possible, talk about how they can help and what they can avoid doing or saying so as not to trigger him or her unnecessarily. Of course, sometimes the children will fail, just as you will fail. You are all human, so talk about it, reestablish the guidelines, give them a hug, and move on. Overreactions will only make the problem worse.

4. Encourage the children to come to you and ask questions and tell you what is going on. Talk to them, but don't make your spouse the "bad guy." Empathize with them and then take the next step. In many cases, they feel helpless and need a solution. As a parent you are the best person to help them solve the problem. Ask them what they need from you. Sit down and make a list of what the two of you can do to change what is going on. Early in my career I used to counsel many children, adolescents, and families. When I asked the kids what they needed most, the young children might shrug, but the adolescents immediately said. "Being understood is great but I need things to change."

See Part Two, Step Three for other problem-solving ideas.

5. Discuss rules and set boundaries for the children, preferably with your mate. Enforce them consistently. You probably set rules and consequences for misbehavior while your mate was gone, but now it is time to discuss those limits with her or him and come to an agreement of exactly what they are. Then talk about how the two of you can handle discipline when necessary. Call a family meeting and let the children know clearly what the rules and consequences are.

Make sure your rules and consequences are rational, and that you are willing and able to enforce them. For instance, say you set a rule, and the consequence for breaking it is that the child or adolescent is grounded and must stay at home after school for the next week, However, both you and your spouse work, so you have no way to make sure that the child is actually at home. In this case, you are asking for trouble. The form of discipline you choose must be one that you can control and enforce. *Be consistent* with implementing the limits you have set. Without consistency, your children learn it's okay for them to break the rules, and that chances are good they'll get away with "bad" behavior.

It is very important that you and your mate support each other in your decisions. If you need to change the rules, try not to criticize each other in front of the children. They must know you are a team and that their parents are in charge. Children need limits and consistency as well as love. It helps them feel secure.

6. Make sure you and your spouse keep your arguments to yourselves. When necessary, take a time-out and find a place by yourselves to argue. Arguments are frightening to children, who are the helpless ones in a family. They are afraid that someone will be violent or will leave and that they have no control over their lives. Often they then bring this anxiety and anger into their school, their homework, and relationships. Or they withdraw into themselves.

7. Don't hesitate to take your children for counseling. If they don't deal with the issues that are bothering them now, the experience may influence them negatively for a lifetime. Often the most effective way to resolve children's issues is to go to counseling as a family, but I realize that is not always possible. Either your spouse or one of the children, frequently an adolescent, will object and refuse to come.

The next most helpful way to resolve children's issues is to have them see the counselor individually at first, and later together with you and your spouse. Children, especially adolescents, need some time of their own with a counselor so they can speak in privacy. The counselor will keep their sessions confidential unless the child wants to tell you what she or he shared in a session. If possible, have some meetings together with your child to help resolve your issues at home.

The Healing Wall
The complete poem

I.

I ignored the Wall -
for a long time.
I had managed to keep out unwanted reminders
of the memories of what I saw and did and felt
and the Wall threatened to violate this self-truce.
For a while, I refused to go to the Wall.
I came close, but I could not bring myself to go down
into that black hole -
So I stood there alone, on the perimeter
of the large descending block of black, cold stone,
and watched from my vantage point on the hill above.

Concealed by the autumn shadows,
hands pocketed, I turned my back and walked away,
mumbling to myself in a voice so low
even I couldn't hear what I was saying,
"Not today, I cannot do this today."

How to Cope with Stress After Trauma

II.

I visited the Wall.
One evening in the late summer of the year,
when the cool winds blew across the Mall and the
early evening sun was crisp, I went to the Wall, again.
I stood where I had stood before but refused to go,
and without ever deciding,
without ever giving consent
I found myself moving toward it,
pulled by some force I could not see,
drawn by memories I could no longer deny.
I began the slow descent into the dark hole,
not wanting to but needing to go back into
what I had spent twenty-five years trying to forget.

At first tentative, I stood next to the first point of the Wall -
looking down the long descent of widening black granite,
wanting to turn back, but I had committed,
this time I needed to go.
I walked down the path, head down,
unable to look up at the Wall -
afraid I would see a name, recognize a name, any name.
Perhaps a name I had seen before, a death I knew before
his family knew. Perhaps a friend, someone who died and
I didn't know.

I couldn't look but I could feel its presence -
as I descended, it cast a silent, shadow, growing on me.
As the sun went down, the darkness deepened.
I stopped where the walk meets in the middle,

The Healing Wall

joining the two parts of the Wall together -
the deepest part of the Memorial
and slowly, my eyes began their climb up the Wall.
Groove by groove, name by name,
I saw what I knew would be there -
names, hundreds and thousands of names
carved into the cold hard flesh of that stone -
first names and last names
carved by the trauma and devastation of the bombs
and the mines and the sniper fire -
and the yells and the screams
of young men dying and not knowing why.
I heard the haunting sound of the death
of all of those soldiers whose
names I had seen and passed on to those places back
home who would receive the telegram
"We regret to inform you..."
I saw the names, blurred as they were,
I saw them and I could not move.

III.

I touched the wall - down in the deep hole where I stood,
I moved forward - not wanting to
but needing to feel it,
needing to trace the edges of at least one name -
not to remember, but to forget.
I touched the smooth stone, gingerly at first, with one finger
feeling the contrast between that and the rough place where the
stone had been violated by the name carved into it -
and in the stillness of that moment

(I remember the stillness, particularly the stillness),
I did what all who go there must do,
I put my whole hand, palm down, against the stone -
first one hand and then the other, softly first,
Then pressing my palm harder against the Wall until
The full weight of my body leaned against it.
Braced by the stone, held up by its quiet, dignified, strength,
I became connected to the Wall,
connected to everything that happened, everything I had felt,
everything I had avoided for over twenty-five years.
Then I was no longer leaning against the Wall,
I was becoming part of the Wall, or the Wall part of me.
The more I tried to pull away, the more I couldn't move.
It began to pull out of me
emotions I had not felt since I was there,
since that first moment I saw and knew
I had been part of someone's death -
reliving the moment of lost innocence,
remembering the emptiness,
feeling again, the sickness in my heart
I had kept numb for years.
That is when the first tear came, and then a second,
followed by more -
slow tears, warm tears from down deep inside the hole of me.
I became a prisoner of the Wall, captive by its silent,
vigilant, roll call of death.

Then I began to move my hands over the Wall -
over names I did not know,
slow at first, and then faster, almost frantically -
at first not knowing why -

The Healing Wall

but then knowing -
I was looking for one name,
I was looking for the one groove my hands
would know the best,
the one that would confirm what I always knew
to be true but was afraid to admit,
a name that wasn't there but should have been -
mine.

It was that sudden realization,
that revelation of surprise,
when it all rushed in,
when it all came back in on me - overwhelming me,
forcing me to face what I had not been able to face before,
the source of my guilt, my one great sin -
I had lived. I had come back home.
I was no more deserving than any one of these names,
but I had survived.
My hands connected to the Wall,
I gave it back - and the Wall took it, all -
the hurt, the pain, the grief, the guilt, the shame.
For the very first time since coming home -
I cried about the War.

These were not slow tears,
they were fast, they were hot and they burned.
I wept for me and I wept for every single family
and town those names, those grooves, touched.
I leaned against the Wall and it held me up
and I finally let go.

When I was empty, out of tears,
the Wall let go and I pulled away.
I looked around and saw others who had done or
were doing the same as I had done.
Each of us in our own way, letting go.
We looked at each other. We didn't speak, but we knew
and shared, in silence.
It was there, beyond the Wall,
I began to heal.

IV.

I left the Wall
I ascended from that deep hole.
Tired, emotionally exhausted,
I looked back where I had been.
I knew my pain had not magically left me -
I carry it with me today -
but I carry it, it no longer carries me.
This was the healing I could not find before -
The Wall told me my name was not there
and said, "Go live your life, you do not belong here."
And so I do, live my life now, beyond the Wall.

As I turned to walk away,
I overheard a small boy,
unaware of war and all its tragedy,
ask his father - "Why are there so many names
on the wall, Daddy?"
and his father's soft reply echoes in my heart, even now -
because I knew he too knew the Wall

the way I knew the Wall -
he replied with the only answer any of us
who have been there have to give -
"I do not know. I do not know."

Epilogue

To this day I do not know why
we have carved so many names on so many walls,
but we have.
What I do know is that there are many casualties of war
we never see carved on walls -
deaths not recorded by grooves chiseled in stone -
kept secret, even from those of us who need to know
the most.
So, as we gather together at this
and all the other walls of war in the world,
let us also honor those of us who lived
with a silent, vigilant, prayer -
a prayer ever present on our lips
and in our hearts...

No more walls, please, no more walls.

© Patrick Overton, PhD, Vietnam veteran
Rebuilding the Front Porch of America

Suggested Readings

Here are a few books that I think might be of particular interest to you. For more suggestions, do an Internet search using terms like, books for veterans with Post Traumatic stress, veterans' experiences, sexual assault in the military, or books to help veteran's families. You will find several books listed online that could be helpful. Also check for veterans' and veterans' families' websites online.

Amen, Daniel G. *Change Your Brain Change Your Life.* Three Rivers Press, New York, New York, 1998
Scientific evidence that your anger, depression, and anxiety could be connected to how different parts of your brain work.

Blum, Sarah. *Women Under Fire: Abuse in the Military.* Brown Sparrow Publishing, Olympia, WA, 2013
A nurse in the Vietnam War, she relates real stories of women who were sexually assaulted in the military.

Castner, Brian. *The Long Walk: A Story of War and the Life that Follows.* Anchor Books, Flushing, MI, 2013
A powerful personal story of a veteran who served on an Ordinance Disposal Unit in Iraq and has PTSD.

Suggested Readings

Cochran, Mark William. *Oby's Wisdom: A Caveman's Simple guide to Holistic Health and Wellness.* Bitterroot Mountain Publishing, Hayden, Idaho, 2012
From his own experience Dr. M. W. Cochran, a veteran, teaches you how to create the holistic mindset and lifestyle that will lead you to a lifelong state of health.

Goodavage, Maria. *Soldier Dogs.* Dutton, Boston, MA, 2012
A leading reporter writes about how military service dogs are trained and what they have accomplished in war. A touching story of heroic dogs who have saved many people.

Maté, Gabor. *When the Body Says No: Understanding the Stress Disease Connection,* John Wiley and Sons, Inc., Hoboken, NJ, 2003
Maté, a medical doctor, reveals and discusses recent scientific evidence that stress effects the body and can create disease. He relates several case studies.

McLay, Robert. *At War with PTSD: Battling Post Traumatic Stress Disorder with Virtual Reality.* Johns Hopkins University Press, Baltimore, MD, 2012
A navy psychiatrist discusses his years of research to create a virtual reality program that can help veterans and military personnel heal from PTSD. He relates the research he has done and his result.

Rothschild, Babette. *8 Keys to Safe Trauma Recovery*, W.W. Norton, New York, NY, 2010
PTSD expert Babette Rothschild lays out eight keys you can use with therapy or without to enhance your healing from trauma.

Seahorn, Janet, and Seahorn, E. Anthony. *Tears of a Warrior.* Team Pursuits, Fort Collins, CO, 2010
A family's story of combat and living with PTSD.

Tick, Edward. *War and the Soul: Healing our Nation's Veterans from Post Traumatic Stress Disorder.* Quest Books, Wheaton, IL, 2005
Tick discusses the spiritual and moral damage of war to veterans and how we can help them heal. He believes that love, compassion, and forgiveness are the key answers. Now also on audio.

Zayfert, Claudia and DeViva, Jason C., *When Someone You Love Suffers from Post Traumatic Stress.* Guilford Press, New York, NY. 2011
Although not written specifically for families and friends of veterans, this is an important book for anyone related to a person who has PTSD.

Acknowledgements

To all the people who have encouraged me, read my drafts, and helped me in the writing of this book, I give a heartfelt thank you. I also thank Jennifer Leo, my editor, and Ronald Goodwin, a nitpicking scientist, who corrected my final manuscript.

I would like to thank all my former teachers, consultants, and clients who have taught me so much about how to cope with the stress that occurs after a severe trauma, and veterans of several wars and their families who have been willing to open up their hearts to me and have spoken honestly about what has and is happening to them.

I am particularly beholden to Patrick Overton, a Vietnam veteran, who has been willing to share his wisdom and his incredible poem with me to help you, the veterans, in the recovery process. I could not have completed this book without him.

About the Author

E. Anna Goodwin M.S, NCC is a former psychotherapist, lecturer, workshop presenter, and writer. In her private practice she specialized in working with clients who came in with symptoms of severe stress after a trauma. Her clients included children, adults, couples, and families who had experienced different traumas such as war, abuse, accidents, and natural disasters. She has taught at two universities, lectured, and conducted a variety of workshops in several states using her extensive knowledge of PTSD.

CPSIA information can be obtained
at www.ICGtesting.com
Printed in the USA
FSOW01n1123010515
6856FS